Exploring Science, LEVEL 3

MILO K. BLECHA
Professor of
Science Education
College of Education
University of Arizona

PETER C. GEGA
Elementary-School
Science Specialist
San Diego State University
San Diego, California

MURIEL GREEN
Supervisor of Science
Board of Education
New York City, Dist. 29
Queens Village, New York

Reviewer/Consultants

Ms. Ruth M. Buck
Teacher, A. Burnet Rhett
Elementary School
Charleston, South Carolina

Lorraine B. Ide
Elementary Science Supervisor
Springfield Public Schools
Springfield, Massachusetts

Imogene C. Moody
Master Teacher/Counselor
Raymond Elementary School
Chicago, Illinois

Cynthia McC. Smith
Teacher, Mitchell
Elementary School
Charleston, South Carolina

Neva Lowe Weaver
Elementary Teacher
Norman Public Schools
Norman, Oklahoma

LAIDLAW BROTHERS • PUBLISHERS

A Division of Doubleday & Company, Inc.

RIVER FOREST, ILLINOIS

Palo Alto, California   Atlanta, Georgia   Dallas, Texas

New York, New York   Toronto, Canada

The Laidlaw Exploring Science Program

Exploring Science LEVEL 1   Exploring Science LEVEL 4

Exploring Science LEVEL 2   Exploring Science LEVEL 5

Exploring Science LEVEL 3   Exploring Science LEVEL 6

Exploring Matter and Energy

Project Director   Thomas E. Navta / *Production Director*   LaVergne G. Niequist / *Art Director*   Gloria J. Muczynski / *Photo Researcher*   William A. Cassin / *Staff Editors*   Sally Wilmot Brown, Helen Fitzpatrick, D. Darragh Smithers, Patricia L. Snyder / *Production Supervisor*   Donna E. Delaine / *Production Associates*   Judith E. Cihock, Cindy L. Jirkovsky, Jamila-Ra, Dee Staahl / *Artists*   Bill and Judi Anderson, Patty Boyd, Paul Hazelrigg, Sid Jordan, Donald Meighan, Larry Mikec / *Cover Design* Donald Meighan

Acknowledgments

The publishers wish to express their appreciation to the following sources for permission to reproduce the photographs on the pages indicated. alfa studio: 13 (top right), 17, 24, 34 (left), 114, 115, 118 (right), 124, 134, 150 (left), 175, 179. Alpha Photo Associates/*Ralph Keller*, 41 (right). Alpha Photo Associates/*Fred M. Doyle*, 45. Alpha Photo Associates/*Wm. T. Littlewood*, 52. Alpha Photo Associates/*Larry P. Trone:* 73, 150 (right), 167. Alpha Photo Associates/*Dana Brown*, 143 (top).

(Acknowledgments continued on page 192)

Copyright © 1976 by **Laidlaw Brothers, Publishers** A DIVISION OF DOUBLEDAY & COMPANY, INC.

ISBN 0-8445-5523-1   PRINTED IN THE UNITED STATES OF AMERICA

123456789 10 11 12 13 14 15   4321098765

CONTENTS

1 Seed Plants

Do you think there are very large trees that grow from very small seeds? Why or why not?

Do you think it is possible to know what kind of plant a seed will grow to be? If so, how?

Where do you think seeds come from?

1 Why are seed plants important?

Were you ever in a park? A field? A forest? If so, think about a time you were there in summer. You may have seen many kinds of plants. Those plants are just some of the many different kinds of plants growing in the world.

Though there are many different kinds of plants, some plants are alike in many ways. One way some plants are alike is that they grow from seeds.

Plants that grow from seeds are called *seed plants*. What are some plants that you think are seed plants?

Food

Seed plants are important to people in many ways. One of these ways is that seed plants are often used for food.

People eat parts of many seed plants. Apples and corn on the cob are parts of seed plants. What other foods do you know of that are parts of seed plants?

People also use parts of seed plants to make food. Bread and peanut butter are such foods. Bread is made from parts of wheat plants. Peanut butter is made from parts of peanut plants.

What other foods do you know of that are made from seed plants? Which seed plants are they made from?

For You to Think About

There are many animals that eat only seed plants. Cows and sheep eat grasses and corn. What other animals do you know of that eat only seed plants? What do you think would happen if there were no seed plants for these animals to eat?

9

Paper is something people use that is made from seed plants. Find out from which seed plants paper is made. Also find out how paper is made. Use reference books to help you. Write a paragraph about what you find out.

Things people use

Seed plants are important to people in another way. That is, many seed plants are used to make things people use.

Look around you. What things do you use that are made of wood? What are some other things made of wood? What kind of seed plant do you think wood comes from?

Many other things people use are made from seed plants. Some of these things are pictured below. Do you think they are important to people? Why or why not?

Beauty

Still another way seed plants are important to people is for their beauty. Some parts of seed plants are green. Many people think this color helps make places look beautiful.

Some seed plants grow flowers. Many people think that flowers look pretty and smell nice. How do you feel when you see and smell flowers?

A Second Look

1. What are seed plants?
2. What are some ways seed plants are important?
3. What are some things people use that are made from seed plants?

11

2 A closer look at seeds

As you may know, there are many kinds of seed plants. And each kind of seed plant makes its own kind of seed. What kinds of seeds have you seen?

How seeds travel

Suppose you could see many kinds of seeds at one time. You would see that each kind looks different. One way seeds look different is their shape.

The shape of many seeds helps them travel. Why do you think seeds must travel?

Look at the pictures below. In what ways are these seeds traveling? Which seeds are helped to travel by their shape? How do you think their shape helps them travel?

Parts of seeds

Though each kind of seed looks different, all seeds are alike in some ways. One of these ways is that seeds are made up of three parts. One part is called the *seed coat*. The seed coat is the outer cover of a seed. Why do you think seeds need to be covered?

The other parts of a seed are found inside the seed coat. One part is a *tiny plant*. The other part is *food* for this plant. Why do you think this food is important?

PARTS OF A CORN SEED

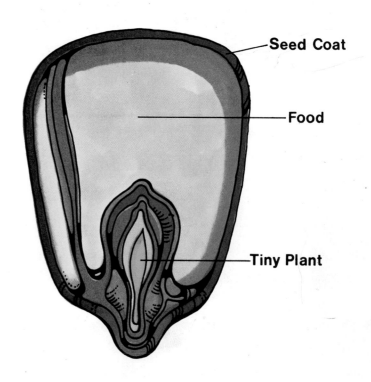

Seed Coat

Food

Tiny Plant

FINDING OUT

What do the insides of some seeds look like?

You will need: 1 or 2 lima beans, 1 or 2 kidney beans, glass of water

▶ Put the seeds (beans are seeds) in the glass of water. Let them soak overnight.
▶ The next day, take the seed coat off each seed.
▶ Break open the seeds.
▶ Draw some pictures showing what the inside of each seed looks like.

What parts of the seeds did you find?
How are these seeds like the seed pictured on page 14? How are they different?

What seeds need to grow

Suppose you wanted some seeds to grow. These seeds would need some things so they could grow. What do you think these things are?

You most likely know of many things you need so that you can grow. Two of these things are air and water. Seeds also need air and water so they can grow.

Along with air and water, seeds need warmth so they can grow. Do you think all seeds need the same amount of warmth? Why or why not?

FINDING OUT

What happens to some seeds without water?

You will need: about 12 seeds, such as lima beans or kidney beans, 2 glass jars, paper towels

► Put half of the seeds in a jar of water. Leave them there overnight.
► The next day, empty the jar and save the seeds.
► Put some paper towels, the seeds, and some water inside the jar as pictured.
► Set up the second jar as you did the first jar, but do not put water in the second jar.
► Leave the seeds in the jars for about a week.
► Look at the first jar every day to see that some water is in it.

What happened to the seeds in the jar with water? Why?
What happened to the seeds in the other jar? Why?

Save the jar of seeds with water in it. You will need the seeds later. Be sure they do not dry out.

A Second Look

1. What are some ways seeds travel?
2. What are the three parts of a seed?
3. What do seeds need so they can grow?

16

What if you were to give a seed everything it needs to grow. You might find that it takes some time for the seed to begin to grow. But after a while, you would see a small plant growing from the seed. This small, young plant is called a *seedling*.

When you take care of a seedling, it should become a full-grown seed plant. How might you take care of a seedling? How might you take care of a seed plant?

3 What do seed plants need to grow?

Air, water, warmth

Like seeds, seed plants need air, water, and warmth so they can grow. But seed plants need other things as well. What do you think these things are?

Though the places in these pictures are different, seed plants can still grow in each place. Why do you think this is so?

Minerals

You may have seen many seed plants. If so, you may know that most of them grow in soil. Seed plants need things which come from soil so they can grow. Some of these things are called *minerals* [MIHN(-uh)-ruhlz]. Do you think some kinds of soil are better than others for seed plants? Why or why not?

For You to Think About

Suppose you had some seed plants growing in a garden. If some weeds started to grow in your garden, what would you do? Why?

Light

Another thing seed plants need so they can grow is *light*. Do you think all seed plants need the same amount of light? Why or why not?

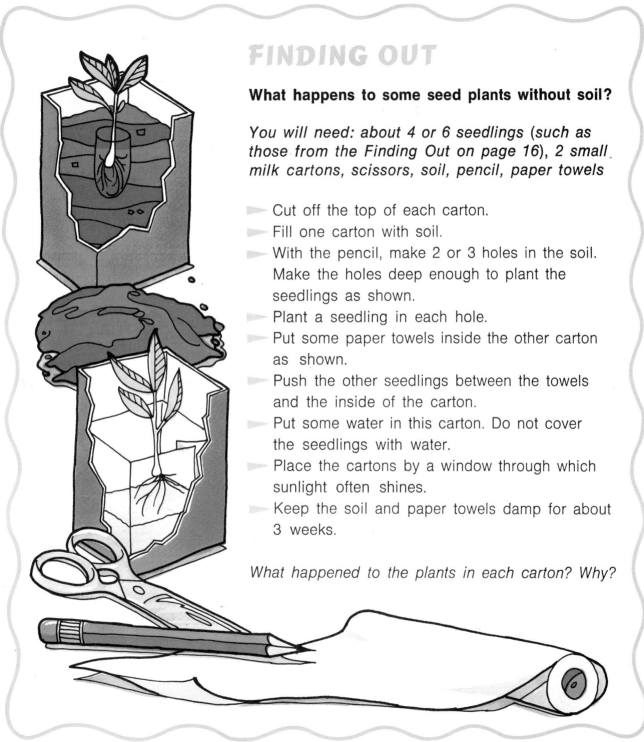

FINDING OUT

What happens to some seed plants without soil?

You will need: about 4 or 6 seedlings (such as those from the Finding Out on page 16), 2 small milk cartons, scissors, soil, pencil, paper towels

> Cut off the top of each carton.
> Fill one carton with soil.
> With the pencil, make 2 or 3 holes in the soil. Make the holes deep enough to plant the seedlings as shown.
> Plant a seedling in each hole.
> Put some paper towels inside the other carton as shown.
> Push the other seedlings between the towels and the inside of the carton.
> Put some water in this carton. Do not cover the seedlings with water.
> Place the cartons by a window through which sunlight often shines.
> Keep the soil and paper towels damp for about 3 weeks.

What happened to the plants in each carton? Why?

FINDING OUT

What happens to some seed plants without light?

You will need: about 4 or 6 seedlings (such as those from the Finding Out on page 16), 2 small milk cartons, scissors, soil, pencil

▶ Cut off the top of each carton.
▶ Fill the cartons with soil.
▶ With the pencil, make 2 or 3 holes in the soil in each carton.
▶ Plant a seedling in each hole as shown.
▶ Place one carton by a window through which the sun often shines.
▶ Place the other carton in a closet.
▶ Keep the soil in both cartons damp for about 2 weeks.

What happened to the plants in each place after about 2 weeks? Why?

A Second Look

1. What is a seedling?
2. What things do seed plants need so they can grow?

20

Have you ever tried to pull weeds out of the ground? If you have, you may know that this is not always easy to do! Weeds, like many other seed plants, are held tightly in the ground. What part of these plants do you think holds them in the ground?

4 Other parts of seed plants

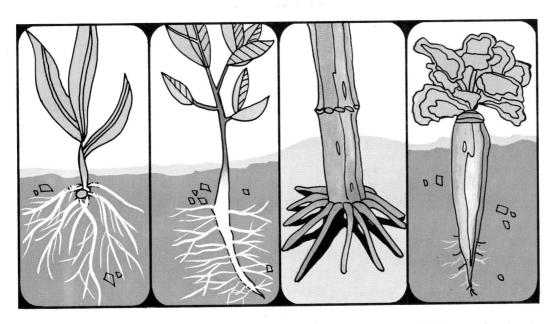

Different kinds of seed plants often have different kinds of roots. How are the roots in the pictures above different?

Root

As you may know, seed plants need water and minerals. These things may be found in the ground. One part of most seed plants grows in the ground. This part is the *root*.

Roots take in water and minerals from the ground. How do you think these things get from the roots to other parts of a seed plant?

Stem

Another part of seed plants is the *stem*. The stem is the part just above the root. The trunk and branches of a tree make up the stem of a tree. Find the stem of the seed plants pictured below. How is the stem of each plant different?

The stem of seed plants is important in many ways. One way is that it carries water and minerals from the root to other parts of the plant. Another way is that the stem holds up other parts of the plant. Why do you think it is important that the stem holds up these other parts?

FINDING OUT

What parts of a stem carry water?

You will need: fresh celery stalk with leaves, a glass, red food coloring, scissors

- Put some water in the glass.
- Put about 4 drops of red food coloring in the glass.
- Cut off the bottom of the celery stalk (celery stalks are stems) as shown.
- Place the celery in the glass.
- After about an hour, take the celery out of the glass.
- Break the celery at about the middle of the stem.
- Look at the inside of the celery where you broke it. Draw a picture of what you see.

Did the leaves or parts of the leaves turn red? If so, how did the red water move through the stem to the leaves?

Leaf

Growing from the stem of seed plants is a part called the *leaf*. The leaf makes food for the plant. The plant uses some of this food to grow. The rest of the food is stored in the plant. When you

23

eat carrots or beets, you are eating roots which are made up of this stored food. Why do you think a seed plant needs to make its own food?

In order to make food, leaves must have water and minerals. Leaves get these things from the stem. They also must have something called *carbon dioxide* [KAHR-buhn dy-AHK-syd]. Carbon dioxide is a part of the air. Leaves put all these things together to make food. Leaves do this with the help of a *green coloring* found inside them and *light*.

Once food is made in the leaves, it mixes with water. Then the food is ready to be used or stored in other parts of the plant. How do you think the food gets to these parts?

Though these kinds of leaves are different in size and shape, they are all able to make their own food. Why?

Flower

Many seed plants have still another part growing from the stem. This part is the *flower*. The flower is the part in which seeds are made. The pictures below show how most seeds are made.

Once seeds are made in the flower, some parts of the flower dry up and fall off. But one

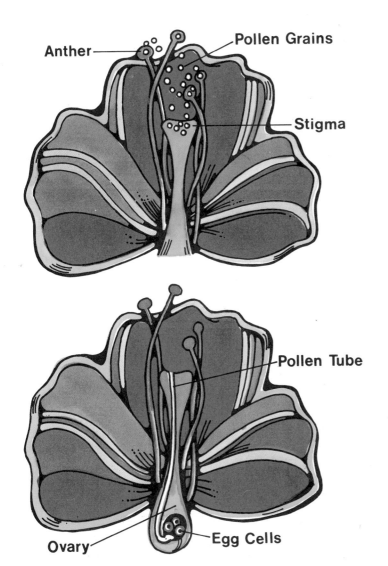

In order for seeds to be made in a flower, pollen grains from the anther must fall on the stigma. Pollen grains from the anther of another flower may land on the stigma of some flowers. How might this pollen get there?

Once a pollen grain lands on the stigma, the pollen grows a tube to the ovary. In the ovary, the pollen joins with an egg cell to become a seed. As the seed grows, the ovary becomes the fruit.

In some seed plants, seeds are not made in flowers. See if you can find out in which parts of these plants seeds are made. Look in reference books under the heading *cone-bearing trees.* Draw pictures to show what you find out.

part of the flower does not dry up and fall off. This part covers the seeds. It is the *fruit.* You may often eat some fruits such as apples. What other fruits do you know of?

Why do you think it is important that the fruit covers the seeds?

FINDING OUT

Can seed plants grow from parts other than seeds?

You will need: white potato, carrot, 2 jars, knife

▶ Cut the potato (white potatoes are stems) into pieces as shown. Make sure that each piece has a spot, or eye, on it.

▶ Cut the carrot (carrots are roots) into pieces as shown.

▶ Place the pieces of stem in one jar. Place the top piece of root in the other jar.

▶ Put some water in each jar.

▶ Look at the jars every day for about a week to see that there is some water in them.

Did the pieces of stem and the piece of root grow? If so, what does this tell you about the ways some plants can grow?

A Second Look

1. What is the root, and why is it important?
2. Why is the stem important?
3. What part of a seed plant makes food, and what things are needed to make the food?
4. Why is the flower important?

Workers Who Use Science

In most parts of the world, people use seed plants for food. To have enough of this food, many people grow seed plants. People who do this for a living are called *farmers.*

Farmers do many things to help seed plants grow. To do these things, farmers use many ideas and practices learned from science. For instance, farmers break up soil before they plant seeds. Farmers know that breaking up soil helps seeds and roots get air and water. Farmers may also put *fertilizer* [FURT-uhl-EYE-zur] in soil. Farmers know that fertilizer gives seed plants minerals the plants may not get from soil.

To find out more about how farmers use science, try to find answers to these questions:

How do farmers keep weeds, insects, and diseases from hurting growing seed plants?
What is plant breeding? Why is it important?
What is crop rotation? Why is it important?
What is irrigation? Why is it important?

Along with sources of your own, writing to the following source may help you: U.S. Department of Agriculture, Office of Information, Washington, DC 20250.

Besides pumpkins, what other seed plants do farmers grow for food?

Reviewing the Main Ideas

Seed plants are important for beauty, food, and
  things people use.
The shape of many seeds helps them travel.
Seeds are made up of a seed coat, a tiny plant,
  and food for this plant.
Seeds need air, water, and warmth so they can
  grow.
Seed plants need air, water, warmth, minerals, and
  light so they can grow.
The root of a seed plant takes in water and minerals.
The stem of a seed plant carries water and minerals
  from the root to other parts of the plant. The
  stem also holds up other parts of the plant.
The leaf of a seed plant makes food for the plant.
The flower is the part of some seed plants in which
  seeds are made.
The seeds of some seed plants are covered by a
  fruit.

Reading About Science

Rahn, Joan Elma. *Seeing What Plants Do*. New York:
  Atheneum Publishers, 1972.
Selsam, Millicent E. *The Apple and Other Fruits*. New
  York: William Morrow & Co., Inc., 1973.
Tinsley, Thomas E. *Plants Grow*. New York: G. P.
  Putnam's Sons, 1971.

Testing for Understanding

On your paper write *T* for each sentence below that is true. Write *F* for each sentence that is false.

1. When you take care of a seedling, it should become a full-grown seed plant.
2. Seeds need water, air, and light so they can grow.
3. The shape of many seeds helps them travel.
4. People use parts of seed plants to make food.
5. Seeds are made in the stem of a seed plant.

Write on your paper the word or words that best fit in each blank below. Choose from these words: *seedling, fruit, stem, carbon dioxide, root, leaf, seed coat, minerals.*

Words to Use

1. The ____ of a seed plant makes food for the plant.
2. Water and minerals are taken in from the ground by the ____ of a seed plant.
3. A ____ is a small, young seed plant.
4. ____ is the part of the air that seed plants need to make food.
5. The part of the flower that covers the seeds is the ____.

Having Fun with Science

What Am I?

1. I make a special food, but I am not a cook.
2. I am a coat, but people cannot wear me.
3. I am a seed plant, but I am not full grown.

Fun with Words

Try to make the letters below into words about seed plants.

tmes   orto

alfe   turif

Things to Do

1. Find out what a greenhouse is. Ask your teacher to help you plan a visit to a greenhouse. Make a list of questions about seed plants you would like answered by someone who works in the greenhouse.

2. Grow your own vegetables. Leave some radish seeds and lettuce seeds in a glass of water overnight. The next day, plant the seeds in some large buckets of soil. If you take care of the seeds and seedlings, you should have radishes and lettuce in about six weeks. Try growing other vegetables.

3. Find two or three different kinds of flowers. Draw a picture of each flower. Then take the flowers apart and draw each part. How are the flowers alike? How are they different?

2 Animal Behavior

What are some other ways animals behave?

What are some things that might make animals behave as they do?

Where have you had fun watching animals?

1 Environment and behavior

Have you ever watched fish? Or a cat? Or a dog? If so, you know animals are often fun to watch. It's fun to watch a dog wag its tail when it is happy. How do you think a cat acts when it is happy?

Each kind of animal has its own way of acting. The way an animal acts is called its *behavior* [bih-HAY-vyur].

Look at the pictures of the animals shown below. How are they behaving? What things in their *environment* [ihn-VY-ruhn-muhnt], or surroundings, might be making them behave as they are?

Heat and behavior

Many things around an animal may make it behave the way it does. One of these things is heat. Things which are warm may make an animal behave one way. Things which are cold may make it behave another way.

Heat "bugs" insects. Maybe you have listened to a cricket chirp. If so, you may know that when the air is warm, a cricket chirps fast. When the air is cool, it chirps more slowly. How do you think heat might make other insects behave?

The skin of this salamander must be kept moist and cool. How might crawling into this hole help the salamander do this?

Something's fishy. Have you ever gone fishing in a lake during summer? If so, you may have caught a fish close to the top of the lake. But what if you were to try to catch the same kind of fish in winter. You might have to fish deeper. Why do you think this might be so?

In summer, the water is warmer at the top of a lake. In winter, the water is warmer down deep. Some fish go to warmer water. Other fish go to cooler water. Why might this be so?

FINDING OUT

How does cooling or warming a goldfish's water change its breathing?

You will need: 1 goldfish in a large glass jar half filled with water (at room temperature), clock with a second hand, thermometer, cold water, warm water

► Write down the temperature of the goldfish's water.
► Write down the number of times the fish breathes in 1 minute. You can find this out by counting how many times its gills open and close.
► Add a little cold water to the jar *slowly.* Do not let the temperature go down more than 5 degrees in 15 minutes, or you may hurt the fish.
► Write down the temperature of the water in the jar.
► Write down the number of times the fish breathes in a minute.

How does cooling the water change the breathing of the goldfish?
What do you think would happen to the breathing of the goldfish if you made the water warmer than room temperature? Try finding out.

Ouch! That's hot! Heat sometimes makes you behave in a certain way. What if you put your hand on a hot pan. You would pull your hand away at once. At what other times might something hot make you behave in a certain way?

What would happen if you were taking a shower and the water suddenly turned cold? You might start to shiver. How else might something that is cold make you behave?

Light and behavior

Another thing which may make an animal behave as it does is light. When have you seen light make an animal behave in a certain way?

Hide and seek. As you may know, some animals move around in daytime. Others move around at night. One animal that moves around at night is the cockroach. Cockroaches feel their way in

Exploring on Your Own

You may have seen moths flying in circles around a light on a summer night. Find out why moths do this. Also find out if other insects do this. You may wish to use reference books. Look under the headings *moths* and *insects*.

What do you think helps this cockroach feel its way in the dark?

38

the dark when looking for food. They do not like light. So when someone turns on a light, they run for cover.

What other animals do you know of that do not like light?

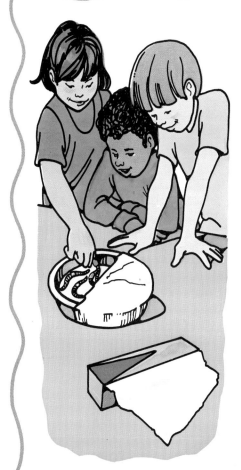

FINDING OUT

What does light make earthworms do?

You will need: about 6 earthworms, pie pan, aluminum foil

▶ Stretch the foil over half of the pie pan. There should be room for the worms to crawl under the foil.

▶ Place the worms in the uncovered part of the pie pan.

Where do the worms go? Why?

▶ Write down the number of worms that move toward light. Write the number of worms that do not.

If you tried this 3 or 4 times, do you think the worms would do the same thing? Try finding out.

Watching eyes. Look at the eyes of someone near you. See how big the pupils of the eyes are. The pupil is the black, round spot in the center of the eye.

Have that person close both eyes for a minute. When the person's eyes are opened, look quickly at the pupils of the eyes. What happened to the pupils while the eyes were closed? What happened to the pupils when the eyes were opened again? Why?

Owls come out at night. How do you think the large pupils in their eyes help them?

Water and behavior

Still another thing which may make an animal behave as it does is water. How do you think water might make some animals behave?

At home on the rocks. Look at the pictures of the animal on this page. It is a *chiton* [KYT-uhn]. It lives on the rocks at the seaside. When the water is high, it covers the animal. The chiton, like a fish, needs to be covered with water so that it can breathe.

When the water is low, it does not cover the animal. The animal becomes dry. What do you think the animal will do so it can keep breathing?

FINDING OUT

How does being wet or dry make an earthworm behave?

You will need: about 6 earthworms, pie pan, 2 paper towels, tape

▶ Place the towels in a pie pan. Do not let the towels touch each other. Hold them down with tape.
▶ Wet one of the towels.
▶ Place half of the worms on the wet towel.
▶ Place the other half on the dry towel.

What do you think will happen?

▶ Watch the worms.

Which way does each worm move? Why?

▶ Try it again.

Do the worms move the same way? Why?

A *mud bath!* If you have ever had a turtle, you know turtles live in water. At times they come out of the water to sun themselves. When they become dry, they go back into the water.

Sometimes a pond may dry up. Turtles in the pond then bury themselves in the mud where

it is wet. They stay covered until it rains. The rain helps them get moving again.

Heat, light, and water are only a few things which make animals behave as they do. What other things around animals make them behave as they do? How do these things make animals behave?

For You to Think About

Earthworms often come out on the sidewalk after a heavy rain. Why do you think they leave their home when the ground is wet?

A Second Look

1. What is meant by animal behavior?
2. What are some things around an animal that may make it behave as it does?

2 Instincts of animals

As you may know, things around an animal may make it behave as it does. Light makes cockroaches run away and hide. Other animals may be drawn to light. Such behavior is very simple.

But what about when a mother bird sits on her eggs to keep them warm? That behavior is not so simple. Yet she does not have to learn to do this. She does this because of an *instinct* [IHN-stihng(k)t]. An instinct is the ability to do something without having to learn how. Animals are born with instincts.

Building things

Instincts may help an animal do many things. An instinct may help an animal build something.

Spider school? You may have seen a spider make a web. Spider webs look hard to make. Yet no one has to teach a spider how to make a web. The first web a spider makes is just right. An instinct helps it make the web. How do you think a web is helpful to a spider?

For You to Think About

Some animals, like many birds, make very strong homes. Other animals, like elephants, make no homes at all. Why do you think some animals do not make homes?

45

Nest making. What if you found a bird's nest. Could you tell what kind of bird made it? All robins make the same kind of nest. Other birds make their own kind of nest. An instinct helps them do this.

Do you think it is important that instincts help animals build things? Why or why not?

FINDING OUT

Can you build a bird's nest as well as a bird?

You will need: mud, twigs, leaves, yarn, newspaper, cup of water

➤ Open the newspaper on a desk or table.
➤ Using the rest of the materials, try to make a bird's nest like the one in the picture.
➤ Let it dry overnight.

What did you find hard to do in making the nest?
If you were to make more nests, do you think you would become better at making them? Why or why not?
Do you think a bird finds it hard to build its first nest? Why or why not?

➤ Compare your nest with the ones made by other people in your class.

Do they look the same? Why or why not?

Guarding their place

Besides helping animals build things, instincts help them do other things. An instinct may help animals guard the place that belongs to them.

Singing guard. Think of the last time you heard a bird sing. You may have thought it was singing because it was happy. But many birds sing to say, "This is *my* place. Stay away, stay away!"

Barking police dog. If you or a friend have a dog, you may have seen how it guards its home. It may bark if someone comes to its home. It may even bark if someone goes by outside. This seems to be its way of saying, "This place belongs to me."

Do you think it is important that animals guard their place? Why or why not?

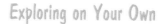

Exploring on Your Own

The ways instincts work have puzzled people for a long time. But people do know some things about instincts. Find out how some instincts are thought to work. Look in a reference book under the heading *instinct*.

Animals sometimes fight for reasons other than guarding the place that belongs to them. Why might these rhinos be fighting?

47

Making trips

Another thing many animals do is travel. Yet they do not plan their trips. How do you think they know when and where to go?

Fish story. Some fish go on very long trips. Salmon are fish that are born in a river. When they are two years old, they swim many miles out to sea. Four years later, they go back to the river where they were born. They go back to lay their eggs. An instinct helps them find their way back.

Birds buzz off. In many places, there are more birds in the summertime than in the wintertime. Where do you think some of the birds go for the winter?

People who study birds put tags on some of them. These tags have an address. If anyone finds a bird with a tag, that person is asked to return the tag to the address. The person is also asked to tell when and where the bird was found. This way it is known where these birds go for the winter. Why do you think it is better for some birds to fly away for the winter?

For You to Think About

Some animals, like salmon, make very long trips. Other animals, like squirrels, do not travel much at all. Why do you think some animals do not travel much?

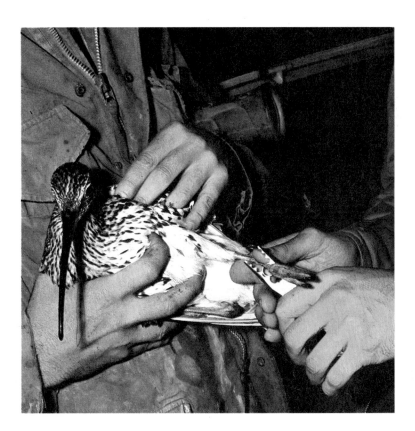

Living together

Sometimes animals live together in a family. This helps the animals in many ways.

Fish families. Some fish protect their baby fish. Bigger fish might eat them. The father fish cares for the babies for a while. The mother fish takes over when he is tired. What do you think makes these fish take care of their baby fish?

Not all animals live in a family as these monkeys and ducks do. What animals do you know of that do not live in a family?

FINDING OUT

How can you watch the behavior of some small animals?

You will need: small animals (such as worms, beetles, and spiders), widemouthed jar with a lid, food wrap, piece of wood, pebbles, sand, small jar lid, stones, small plants, soil

➤ Cut the piece of wood as shown. Lay the jar on its side with the neck resting on the wood.

➤ Place a layer of small pebbles in the jar.

➤ Add a layer of sand. Put the small jar lid in the sand as a pond. Put some water in it.

➤ Add some soil, stones, small plants, and a twig or two.

➤ Put holes in the lid of the jar.

➤ Cover about half the mouth of the jar with food wrap. Put the lid on the jar.

➤ Put the jar in a cool place (about 18°C or 65°F).

➤ Let it stand for 2 or 3 days. If the sides are very wet, you need fewer plants or more air.

➤ Add the animals you want to watch. Also add any food they might need.

Which animals like to get under things?
Which animals like to move about?
What other kinds of animal behavior do you see?
Why do you have to know something about an animal's behavior when keeping it in a jar?

Bird feeders. Have you ever watched baby birds eat? If so, you know baby birds need very much food. In fact, both the father and mother must work together to get enough food for the babies. Later, some birds teach their little ones to find their own food. They do all these things by instinct.

How else might instincts help animals living in a family?

A Second Look

1. What is meant by an instinct?
2. Why are instincts important to animals?
3. What are some instincts that animals have?

If you have ever watched a newborn puppy, you know it can do very little. But it can do some things. As soon as it is born, it can snuggle to its mother to get warm. And it knows by instinct how to get food from its mother.

But a puppy soon *learns* to do many things. That is, it finds out how to do things it could not do before. It learns how to find its way back to its "home" corner if put into another corner. It learns to play with a ball. What other things might a puppy learn?

3 Animals can learn, too!

What things do you think this newborn lamb will have to learn?

What the senses, nerves, and brain do

Many parts of the body help an animal to learn. What if you gave a puppy something new for supper. First, it would *smell* the food. Messages about how it smells would be sent along a nerve from the nose to the brain. Then, the puppy would *taste* the food. Messages about how it tastes would be sent along a nerve from the tongue to the brain.

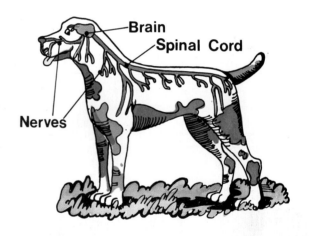

Smelling and tasting are senses which help the animal learn about this new food. The next time it is given that food, the puppy will remember if it likes the food or not. What other senses might help animals learn?

Do you think all animals can learn? Which animals seem to learn better than others? Why do you think this is so?

How animals learn

Animals learn about things in many ways. What ways can you think of that animals learn?

Watching others. As you may know, some animals must hunt for their food. Young lions watch their mothers hunt for food. They see the best ways to catch another animal. When they get older, they know how to hunt. They have learned by watching their mothers hunt.

What else might animals learn by watching others?

What have you learned by watching others?

Exploring on Your Own

Watch someone tie his tie. What does he do first? Try following the steps. See if you can learn to do it just by watching him.

These puma cubs are getting a lesson in hunting. What are some things you think they must learn about hunting?

55

Trying one way, then another. Animals also learn by trying things out. An ant may not be able to find its way back to its nest. Someone may have cleaned around the nest. This may erase the trail that the ant has left. It has to try new ways to get home. It will try one way, then another. At last it may find its nest.

What have you learned by trying something one way and then another?

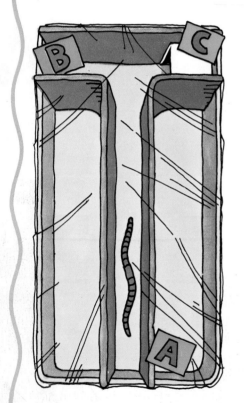

FINDING OUT

Can an earthworm learn to find its way home?

You will need: earthworm, tray, clear food wrap, clay, small note card, paper towel

➤ Using the clay, build a path for the worm in the tray as shown.
➤ Make a house for the worm out of the note card.
➤ Put the worm at A. Put the house over it.
➤ To begin, move the house to C. Quickly cover the tray with food wrap.
➤ Find out how many times it takes the worm to find its home at C. Let the worm rest on a wet paper towel 5 minutes after each run.

Did your worm learn to find its way home? If so, how do you know?

Doing things over and over. Another way animals learn is by doing something over and over. When a squirrel opens its first nut, it is hard work. After opening many nuts, the squirrel finds the best way to open a nut. Then it is easy for the squirrel.

What other things do animals learn by doing them over and over?

What have you learned by doing something over and over?

Learning one thing because of another. As you may know, animals get their food in many ways. Toads like to catch flies. There is a fly that looks just like one kind of bee. It is the robber fly. If a toad eats a robber fly, it has a good dinner. But if it tries to eat a bee, it gets stung. Toads stay away from bees. Some toads also stay away from robber flies. Why might this be so?

For You to Think About

You may have heard that people sometimes learn from their mistakes. What have you learned in this way?

In what ways does the robber fly on the left look like the bees on the right?

Many times, a dog will know which cupboard its food is kept in. What if someone opens the door of that cupboard. The dog will get excited and wag its tail. It will do these things even before it sees or smells the food! The dog has learned that when the door is opened, "dinner" is coming.

What things have you learned because of something else?

FINDING OUT

How can a fish learn to do one thing because of another?

You will need: 2 or 3 fish in a bowl of water, fish food

► Tap the side of the bowl 3 times.

What, if anything, do the fish do?

► Just before you feed the fish each day, tap the bowl 3 times.
► Do this for about 10 days.
► On the eleventh day, tap 3 times on the bowl. But do not feed the fish.

What do the fish do? Why?

Working out problems. Some animals can learn by working out problems. The picture on this page shows a dog that cannot get to its food. Some dogs can work out a way to get to the food. They can see they must back up and go around the post. What else might they try to do to get the food?

Though some animals can work out problems, people are better at doing this. You can do puzzles. You can do math problems. What games do you play in which you have to work out problems?

A Second Look

1. What is learning?
2. What parts of the body help an animal to learn?
3. What are some ways animals learn?

Workers Who Use Science

Many people like to watch how animals behave. There are some workers who must know much about animal behavior. One such worker is the *animal keeper* at the zoo.

An animal keeper must know how much light, heat, and water each kind of animal needs. For example, some animals like to stay in a dark place for part of the day. An animal keeper must be sure these animals have such a place to go.

An animal keeper must also know about an animal's instincts. The keeper must know that putting two male birds of the same kind too close together might make them fight. What other instincts must the animal keeper know about?

To find out more about animal keepers, try to find the answers to these questions:

What else must animal keepers know about animal behavior?

How do animal keepers feed many kinds of animals such as giraffes and elephants?

What things might an animal keeper do to help a sick animal?

Along with sources of your own, the following book might be helpful: *Childcraft—The How and Why Library*, Volume 5, *About Animals*. Chicago: Field Enterprises Educational Corporation, 1973, pp. 256–273.

Reviewing the Main Ideas

The way an animal acts is called its behavior.

Things around an animal such as light, heat, and water may make an animal behave as it does.

An instinct is the ability to do something without having to learn how.

Animals may have an instinct for building things, guarding their place, traveling, or living together.

Learning is finding out how to do things that you could not do before.

The senses, nerves, and brain help an animal learn.

Animals learn in many ways.

Reading About Science

Childcraft—The How and Why Library, Volume 5, *About Animals.* Chicago: Field Enterprises Educational Corporation, 1973.

Fritch, Michael. *Some of Us Walk, Some Fly, Some Swim.* Westminster: Random House, Inc., 1971.

Webb, Clifford. *All Kinds of Animals.* New York: Frederick Warne and Co., 1970.

Testing for Understanding

On your paper write *T* for each sentence below that is true. Write *F* for each one that is false.

1. Water sometimes makes animals behave as they do.
2. Some animals know how to build homes without having to learn how.
3. Cockroaches like light.
4. An instinct helps some animals travel.
5. Warm air makes crickets chirp faster than cool air.

Write on your paper the word that best fits in each blank below. Choose from these words: *brain, senses, instinct, nerves, behavior, learning, light.*

Words to Use

1. The way an animal acts is called its ____.
2. The ability to do something without having to learn how is called an ____.
3. Finding out how to do something you could not do before is called ____.
4. Smelling and tasting are ____ which help animals learn.
5. Messages go to the brain along ____.

Having Fun with Science

I am a pupil that never learns, but I behave well without a teacher.

A turtle named Myrtle
Went over a hurdle.

A snake they called Jake
Could not stay awake.

Fun with Words

Try to make up some other jingles. They should tell about animal behavior.

Things to Do

1. Collect about 10 ants. Place them in a shoe box without a lid. Darken the room and turn on a flashlight. Shine the light on the ants. Watch how the light makes the ants behave.

2. Find out if some of the birds near you go away for the winter. If they do, try to find out when and where they go. Find out when they come back. Keep a chart of other interesting things you find out about them.

3. Visit a pet store or watch some fish in an aquarium. See how some fish guard their place in the water. If you are in a pet store, watch the behavior of other animals in the store.

3 Heat and Temperature

What might make Stanley's supper get cold?

What might make Stanley's milk get warm?

What other things do you know of that might become cold or warm? Why might they become cold or warm?

1 Where does heat come from?

Heat is all around you.
It helps you many ways.
Heat cooks your food at suppertime.
It warms you nights and days.

Where does heat come from?
It comes from near and far.
You can make it with your hands
Or get it from a star!

Heat from a star

The poem on page 66 says many things about heat. One thing it says is that heat can come from a star. That star is the sun. When do you feel heat from the sun?

As you may know, the sun can heat many things. It can heat the earth. It can heat the air around you. Why do you think this is important?

FINDING OUT

How can you tell that heat comes from the sun?

You will need: 3 or 4 pairs of small things such as rocks, pieces of aluminum foil, and cups of water

▶ Place one thing from each pair in the sunlight.
▶ Place the other thing from each pair in the shade. Keep all the things away from heaters.
▶ After about an hour, feel each pair of things.

Which things are warmer—the ones in the sunlight or the ones in the shade? Why?

Sometimes you may want heat that is made from rubbing. On a cold day, you might rub your hands to get them warm. But sometimes heat from rubbing is not wanted. Find out when heat from rubbing is not wanted. You may want to use reference books to help you. Look under the heading *heat* or *friction*.

Heat from rubbing

Rub your hands together about ten times. Rub hard and fast. Feel the heat!

Try rubbing other things together. Which of these things can make heat when they are rubbed? What other things do you think can make heat when they are rubbed?

Heat from electricity

Think about some things that make heat in your home. A toaster makes heat to toast your bread. An iron makes heat to iron your clothes. How do you think toasters and irons make heat?

Toasters and irons must be plugged into an outlet to work. They must be plugged in to get *electricity* [ih-LEHK-TRIHS-uht-ee]. It is this electricity that makes heat. Look at the picture below to see how this happens.

What other things do you know of that make heat from electricity?

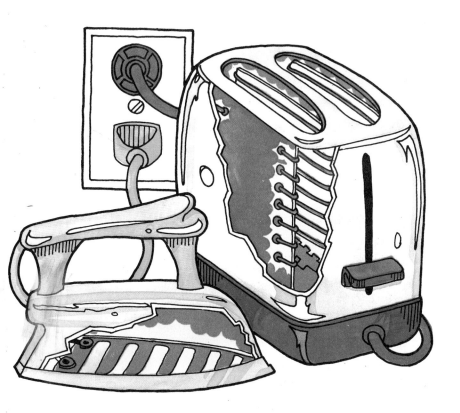

Toasters and irons have special wires in them. When electricity passes through these wires, they get hot. How might you know when toasters and irons are hot?

You may have read about the heat around you. Your body also has heat. This heat comes from inside your body. Find out how your body makes heat. Also find out why this heat is important. You might ask a doctor or your school nurse to help you.

Heat from burning

Look at the pictures below and on the next page. Which of the things shown are giving off heat? Why?

Heat from burning is used in many homes. How might people use this heat in their homes?

Heat from burning is also used in factories. It is used to make many things. Steel for cars is made by using heat from burning. Windows are also made by using heat from burning. What other things do you know of that are made by using heat from burning?

71

In a geyser (left), heat from the earth forces water and steam through a hole in the earth. In a volcano (right), heat forces gases and melted rock through a hole in the earth. Which do you think is hotter? Why?

Heat from the earth

As you may know, most heat comes from above the ground. But some heat comes from deep inside the earth.

Heat from the earth sometimes comes up through openings in the ground. One kind of opening is called a *volcano* [vahl-KAY-noh]. Another kind is called a *geyser* [GY-zur].

People can use this heat from the earth. It can be used to make electricity. Why might this be important?

A Second Look

1. What are some ways in which heat is important?
2. How can you make heat with your hands?
3. What are volcanoes and geysers?

Think about a warm, sunny day. If you were in sunlight, you might feel warm. But suppose you were to walk into the shade. Do you think you would become cold? Why or why not?

Heat moves in air

You may not always be in sunlight or near other things that give off heat. But you can still feel heat from these things. Heat can move in air. Why do you think this is important?

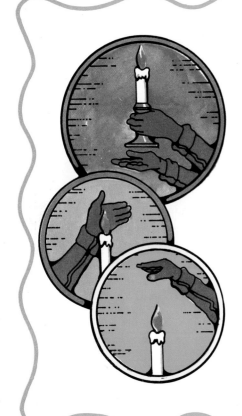

FINDING OUT

Where does the heat from a candle go?

You will need: candle, candleholder, matches

▶ Place the candle in the holder. Be sure it is held tightly in place.
▶ Light the candle.
▶ Place your hand below the flame as shown.
▶ Place your hand next to the flame as shown.
▶ Place your hand above the flame as shown.

Where did you feel the most heat? Why?

Think about your kitchen when the oven is turned on. Heat from the oven warms some of the air around it. As this air becomes warm it rises.

As the warm air rises cool air in the room moves down. It also moves to the oven. This cool air then becomes warm and rises. In this way, heat from the oven keeps moving to other parts of the room. Look at the first drawing on page 75 to see how this happens.

For You to Think About

If you were to look in many rooms, you would find that the heat most often comes from a place in the floor or close to the floor. Why do you think this is so?

Heat makes water in the pan below move in the same way it makes air in the room above move. As water is heated (red arrows), it rises. The cooler water (blue arrows) moves down. How do you know when all the water is heated?

FINDING OUT

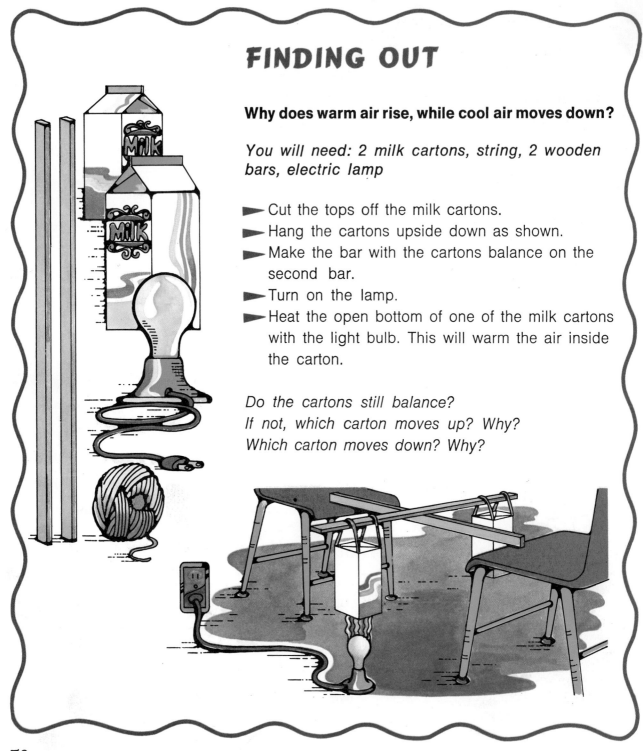

Why does warm air rise, while cool air moves down?

You will need: 2 milk cartons, string, 2 wooden bars, electric lamp

► Cut the tops off the milk cartons.
► Hang the cartons upside down as shown.
► Make the bar with the cartons balance on the second bar.
► Turn on the lamp.
► Heat the open bottom of one of the milk cartons with the light bulb. This will warm the air inside the carton.

Do the cartons still balance?
If not, which carton moves up? Why?
Which carton moves down? Why?

76

Heat moves through objects

Have you ever cooked something in a pan? If so, you may know that the whole pan does not become warm right away. First, the bottom of the pan gets warm. Then, heat moves through the bottom to the sides. Heat may even move through the sides to the handle.

What are some other objects you know of that heat can move through?

Heat can also move from one object to another. If you put a hot cup of soup on a table, heat from the cup would move to the table. At what other times might heat move from one object to another?

FINDING OUT

How does heat move through a coat hanger?

You will need: candle, matches, coat hanger

► Support the hanger above the candle as shown.
► Drip candle wax on the hanger in 3 or 4 places.
► Light the candle. Heat one end of the hanger.

Does heat move through the hanger? If so, how can you tell where the heat has moved?

Keeping heat from moving

Some things are better than others in keeping heat from moving. Find out which of these things might be used to keep heat from moving: water, metal, rubber, glass, cement, cloth, air, and wood. You may wish to use reference books. Look under the heading *heat insulation* or *heat conduction.*

When you are cold, you may want heat to move. You may want it to move from a heater to you. When else might you want heat to move?

Sometimes, however, you may want to keep heat from moving. If you put a hot pan on a table, what might happen to the table? Why? At what other times might you want to keep heat from moving?

There are many things you can use to keep heat from moving. Suppose you wanted to pick up a hot pan. What things might you use to keep the heat from burning your hand?

These children are wearing clothing that keeps heat from moving. Where is the heat coming from that is keeping them warm? How else does their clothing help keep them warm?

People who build homes and other buildings know how to keep heat from moving. They know how to make buildings so that heat does not move through the walls. When would you want heat to stay inside a building? When would you want heat to stay outside a building?

Between the inside and outside walls of this building is a layer of insulation. How does the insulation help keep air inside the building comfortable in summer and winter?

A Second Look

1. How do warm air and cool air move in a room?
2. What are some objects heat can move through?
3. When might you want to keep heat from moving?

3 How heat changes things

Think about the last time you put butter on a hot roll. Heat from the roll warmed the butter. How did the butter change when it became warm?

Heat can change other things too. What other things have you seen changed by heat? How have they changed?

Heat melts things

Suppose you held some ice in your hand. Heat from your hand would change the ice. The ice would change to water. This kind of change is called *melting*.

Heat can melt many things. What are some other things you can think of that heat can melt?

Heat boils things

There is another way in which heat can change things. Suppose you were heating some water on a stove. If you were to add enough heat, the water would change to steam. This kind of change is called *boiling*.

Heat can boil other things too. What are some other things you can think of that heat can boil?

In what ways is food being kept warm in this picture? What are some other ways in which people might keep food warm?

Heat makes things take up more room

Have you ever played on a sidewalk? If so, you may have seen spaces, or cracks, every few feet. People who build sidewalks leave these spaces. These people know that a sidewalk takes up more room when it is warm than when it is cold. The spaces in a sidewalk allow for it to take up more room on a hot day.

There are many other things which take up more room when they are heated. Which of these things can you think of?

For You to Think About

What do you think might happen to a sidewalk on a hot day if builders had not left spaces in it? Why?

The spaces in this bridge allow the bridge to take up more room when it becomes heated. What things do you think cause the bridge to become heated?

83

FINDING OUT

Does heat make air take up more room?

You will need: 2 empty soda bottles, pan of water, source of heat, bowl of ice, 2 balloons

▶ Put the balloons over the necks of the bottles.
▶ Place one bottle in the pan of water. Heat the water.
▶ Place the other bottle in the bowl of ice.

What happens to the air in each balloon? Why?

A Second Look

1. In what ways does heat change things?
2. How does ice change when it melts?
3. How does water change when it boils?

84

Suppose you got letters from two friends. One friend was in Florida. The other was in Alaska. They both wrote telling you that it was a cold day. What if they both wanted to go outside. Do you think one would put on more clothing than the other? Why or why not?

4 Measuring temperature

What is temperature?

You most likely use words like "hot" and "cold" to tell about many things. Feeling something with your hands is one way of telling whether it is hot or cold. This is one way to *measure* [MEHZH-ur] how hot or cold something is. But things which feel hot to you may not feel hot to someone else. And things which feel cold to you may not feel cold to someone else. Why might this be so?

FINDING OUT

Does warm water always feel warm?

You will need: 3 flat pans

▶ Fill one pan with hot water. (Not *TOO* hot)
▶ Fill another pan with cold water.
▶ Fill the last pan with warm water.
▶ Put one hand in the hot water and the other hand in the cold water.
▶ After about 3 minutes, put both hands in the warm water.

Does the water in the third pan feel the same to both hands? If not, which hand feels warm? Why? Which hand feels cool? Why?

If you wanted to know just how hot or cold something is, you would have to find out its *temperature*. The temperature of something tells you just how hot or cold it is.

Temperature is measured in *degrees* [dih-GREEZ]. Something that is hot will measure more degrees than something that is cold.

When you are well, your temperature is about 37 degrees Celsius (98 degrees Fahrenheit). The drawing on this page shows what is meant by Celsius and Fahrenheit. Water boils when its temperature is 100 degrees Celsius (212 degrees Fahrenheit). What do you think is the temperature of the air around you?

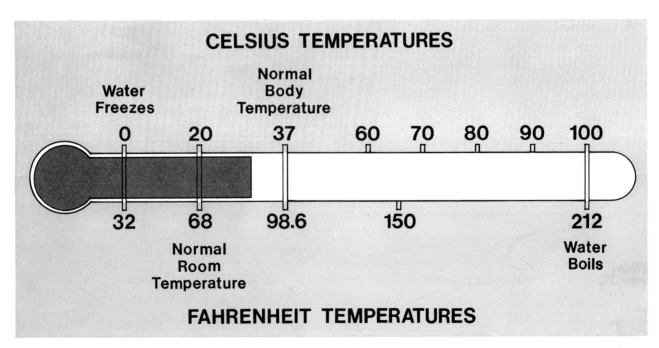

CELSIUS TEMPERATURES

Water Freezes

Normal Body Temperature

0 20 37 60 70 80 90 100

32 68 98.6 150 212

Normal Room Temperature

Water Boils

FAHRENHEIT TEMPERATURES

What is a thermometer?

The best way to measure temperature is to use a *thermometer* [thuh(r)-MAHM-uht-ur]. Look at the thermometers pictured on this page. These thermometers show the air temperature of two rooms. You can read each thermometer by finding where the top of the red line ends. What number is at the end of each red line? Which room is the warmer?

The symbol °C is often used to show degrees Celsius. And the symbol °F is often used to show degrees Fahrenheit. Why do you think these symbols are used instead of the words?

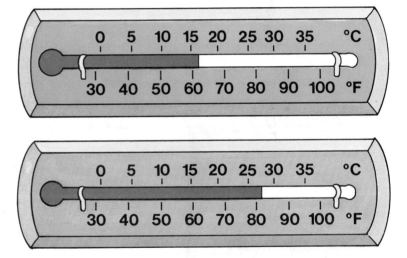

The red line in these thermometers is a red *liquid* [LIHK-wuhd]. This liquid is in a glass tube. When these thermometers were made, the liquid was put in the bulb at the bottom of each tube.

When heated, the red liquid in a thermometer is like most other things. That is, it will take

88

up more room when it is warm than when it is cool. So, when the red liquid is heated, it will rise in the tube. When the red liquid is cooled, it will fall in the tube.

FINDING OUT

Can you "watch" the temperature of things change?

You will need: 3 jars, 4 thermometers

▶ Write down the temperature of each thermometer.
▶ Fill one jar with hot water, one with ice water, and one with warm water.
▶ Put one thermometer in each jar. Leave one thermometer out in the air.
▶ Write down the temperature of each thermometer every 3 or 4 minutes. Do this for about 15 minutes.

How did each thermometer change?
Which one shows the highest temperature? Why?
Which one shows the lowest temperature? Why?

▶ Guess the temperature of different things around you. Then measure them.

How close were your guesses?

There are many other kinds of thermometers. Some are shown on this page and the next. Which kinds of thermometers have you seen?

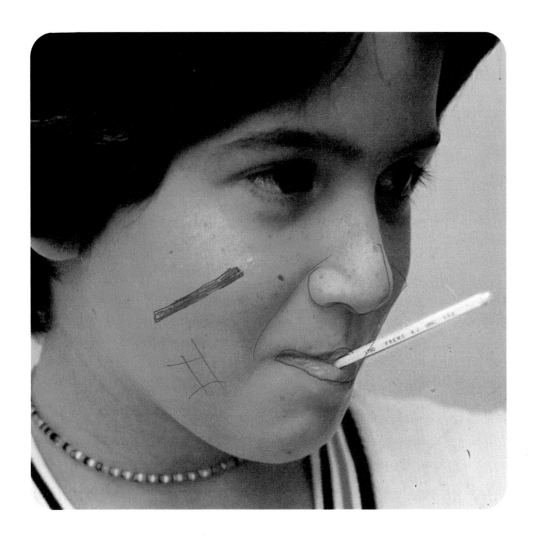

A Second Look

1. Why is feeling something with your hands not the best way to measure its temperature?
2. What does the temperature of something tell you?
3. What is the best way to measure temperature?

Workers Who Use Science

Many times, heat from burning is helpful. You might cook or keep warm with this heat. Other times heat from burning is not wanted. Every year, many things are burned in fires.

Many people work to keep fires from starting or spreading. These people are called *fire department workers. Fire inspectors* are fire department workers who look in buildings to help make sure fires will not start. They make sure that things which might catch fire are not close to heaters. They also look for things which might start fires, such as worn electric wires.

Fire fighters are fire department workers who know how to put out fires after they start. These people sometimes have to go through rooms filled with smoke and heat. They know that hot air rises. By keeping down low, they may get to the fire and put it out.

To find out more about fire department workers, try to find answers to these questions:

What do fire fighters wear to protect themselves?
What do fire department workers teach others about preventing fires?
What is used to put out different kinds of fires?

Along with sources of your own, visiting or writing to a local fire department may be helpful.

Reviewing the Main Ideas

Heat comes from the sun, rubbing, electricity, the
  earth, and burning.
Heat moves in air.
Warm air rises, while cool air moves down.
Heat can move through objects.
Heat can move from one object to another.
There are many things you can use to keep heat
  from moving.
Heat can melt and boil some things.
Most objects take up more room when they are
  warm than when they are cool.
The temperature of something tells you just how
  hot or cold it is.
Temperature is measured in degrees.
The best way to measure temperature is to use a
  thermometer.

Reading About Science

Adler, Irving, and Adler, Ruth. *Heat and Its Uses*.
  New York: The John Day Company, 1973.
Barratt, D. H. *Heat*. Discovering Science Series.
  New York: World Publishing Company, 1972.
Cobb, Vicki. *Heat*. New York: Franklin Watts, Inc.,
  1973.
Simon, Seymour. *Hot & Cold*. New York: McGraw-
  Hill Book Company, 1972.
Urquhart, David I. *Central Heating & How It Works*.
  New York: Henry Z. Walck, Inc., 1972.

Testing for Understanding

Ideas to Check

On your paper, write *T* for each sentence below that is true. Write *F* for each sentence that is false.

1. All heat comes from the sun.
2. Warm air rises.
3. Heat cannot move through objects.
4. Heat can change water to steam.
5. Most things take up more room when they are warm than when they are cool.

Words to Use

Write on your paper the word that best fits in each blank below. Choose from these words: *boiling, geysers, rubbing, thermometer, heat, melting, volcanoes, electricity, measuring.*

1. You can make heat by ____ your hands together.
2. When you plug in a toaster, you get heat from ____.
3. Heat comes from the ground through openings called ____ and ____.
4. Ice can change to water. This change is called ____.
5. Water can change to steam. This change is called ____.
6. The best way to measure temperature is to use a ____.

Having Fun with Science

1. I am water, but I am not wet.
2. I go up chimneys, but I do not come down chimneys.
3. I am a star you never see at night.

Brainteasers

1. There are many liquids used in thermometers. But no one wants to use water. Why?

2. People in hot places often wear light-colored clothing. Why? People in cold places often wear dark-colored clothing? Why?

Fun with Words

thermo + meter = heat + measure = thermometer
Thermo and *therm* mean "heat." What do you think the following things are?

thermos bottle   thermal underwear

Find other words that begin with *therm*.

Things to Do

1. When you stand in sunlight, you make a shadow. Heat cannot be seen. Does it make a shadow? Shine a flashlight on a wall. Hold a candle in front of the light. Does the candle make a shadow? Light the candle. Is there another shadow? If so, what is making this shadow?

2. Invent your own ice-cube keeper. See how long you can keep heat from melting ice. Use things that will keep heat out.

4 Sounds Around You

How might some sounds make you feel?

Why do you think it is important to hear sounds around you?

1 How are sounds alike?

Listen to the sounds around you. Do you hear someone talking? Or a car going by? Or maybe a dog barking? If not, what sounds do you hear?

Making sounds

Most sounds you hear are different from one another in some ways. Some sounds are loud. Others are soft. In what other ways are sounds different from one another? Do you think that sounds are alike in any ways? If so, how?

Sounds made by objects. Many objects, or things, around you make sounds. But for an object to make a sound, one important thing must be happening to it. The object or part of it must be *vibrating* [VY-BRAYT-ihng], or moving back and forth very fast. What objects have you seen or felt vibrating fast enough to make a sound?

Look at the picture on this page. Which objects do you think are making a sound? Why?

For You to Think About

Many sounds you hear are important to you. Make a list of the sounds you heard today. In what ways are these sounds important to you? What are some other sounds that might be important to you? Why might they be important?

FINDING OUT

Can you see how a sound is made?

You will need: wooden ruler or piece of wood about the size of a ruler

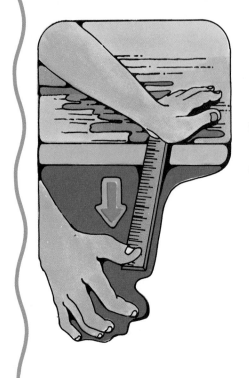

- Hold one end of the ruler firmly on a table as shown.
- Push down on the other end of the ruler with your thumb.
- Quickly slide your thumb off the end of the ruler.

What do you hear?

- Try it again. Watch the ruler very carefully.

What is happening to the ruler while it is making a sound?

Sounds made by your voice. Place three fingers on your throat. Place them on top of the "bump" in your throat. Hum something. What did you feel? Do you think you have found where your voice sounds are made? Why or why not?

The bump you felt is your *voice box.* Inside your voice box are two important things. They are called *vocal cords* [VOH-kuhl KAWRDZ]. The picture on this page shows what the vocal cords look like. Why do you think your vocal cords are important?

When you talk, you breathe out. And as you breathe out, air passes between your vocal cords. What do you think air does to your vocal cords to make sounds?

As you may know, humming and talking are some voice sounds you make. What are some other voice sounds you make? Do you think you use your vocal cords to make these sounds? How might you find out?

For You to Think About

As you may know, when you make voice sounds, you breathe out. But why do you think you do not make voice sounds every time you breathe out?

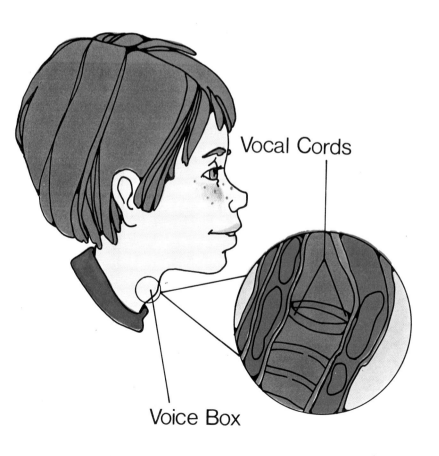

Vocal Cords

Voice Box

FINDING OUT

How do your vocal cords make sounds?

You will need: toy balloon

Because your vocal cords are inside your body, you cannot see them make sounds. But you can use a balloon to help show how vocal cords work.

▶ Fill the balloon with air. Hold it as shown.
▶ Stretch the mouth of the balloon by pulling on each side. At the same time, let some air out.
▶ Watch the sides of the balloon at the opening.

What do you see?
What do you hear?
What do you think is making the sound?
Why?
How do you think your vocal cords
and the sides of the balloon are alike?

Travels of sounds

You most likely know that sounds are alike in how they are made. But sounds are also alike in how they travel.

Up, down, all around? Suppose some friends were standing in a circle around you. If you were to clap your hands above your head, your friends would most likely hear the clapping sound. This is because the sound would travel in the direction of each person in the circle. In what other directions do you think the sound would travel?

FINDING OUT

In what directions can sound travel?

You will need: 2 metal spoons, piece of string

➤ Tie one end of the string to a spoon.
➤ Have a partner hit this spoon with the other spoon as you walk in a circle around your partner.

Could you hear the sound of the spoon from any place in the circle?

➤ Have your partner sit on the floor. Stand so that your head is above the spoon.
➤ Have your partner hit the spoons together.

Did you hear the sound of the spoon?

➤ Sit on the floor. Have your partner hit the spoons together above your head.

Did you hear the sound of the spoon?
In what directions can sound travel?

As you may know, sounds can travel through many things. See if you can find out how sounds travel through things. To do this, you might use reference books. Look under the heading *sound* or *sound waves.*

Through air, water, and other things? Most sounds you hear reach you by traveling through air. But sounds can also travel through other things.

Look at the pictures on this page. Through what things is sound traveling? What do you think are some other things sounds travel through?

FINDING OUT

How can you make a string telephone?

You will need: 2 paper cups, about 4 metres (13 feet) of string, sharp pencil

➤ Make a small hole in the center of the bottom of each cup with the pencil.

➤ Put one end of the string through the bottom of one of the cups as shown.

➤ Tie a knot in the end of the string.

➤ Do the same thing with the other paper cup.

➤ Get a partner and hold the cups as the children are doing in the picture. Be sure to keep the string straight.

➤ Whisper something to your partner through your "telephone." Have your partner whisper to you. If you did not hear each other, try whispering a little louder.

Did your telephone work? If so, how did your voice reach your partner's ear?

A Second Look

1. In what ways are sounds alike?
2. How are sounds made?
3. In what ways do sounds travel?

2 Hearing sounds

Bang! Pop! Buzz! Splash! As you may know, these sounds and others can travel through many things to reach your ears. Look at the drawing below. What do you think happens to these sounds so that you can hear them?

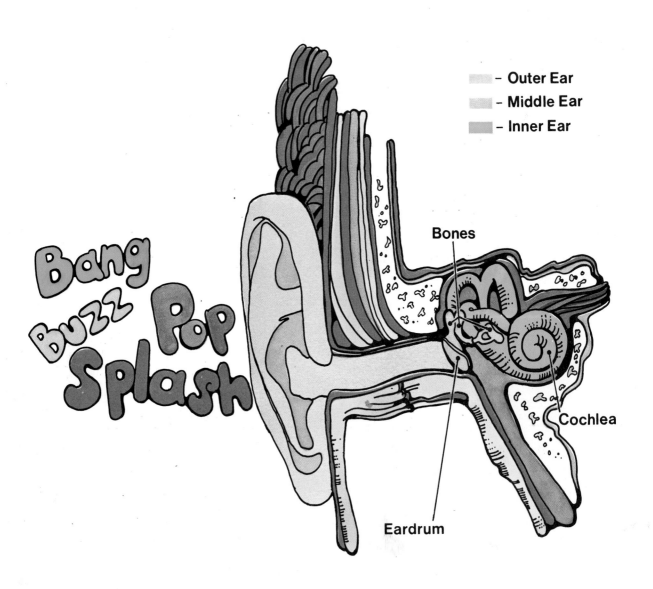

- Outer Ear
- Middle Ear
- Inner Ear

Bones

Cochlea

Eardrum

How do you hear sounds?

Try "wiggling" your ears. Can you do it? Some people can. Some people cannot.

Outer ear. The part of the ear some people can wiggle is one part of the *outer ear.* The outer ear has another part. This part is a small tunnel. Look at someone's ears. You can see the opening to this tunnel.

One thing the outer ear does is "catch" sounds. It also carries these sounds into another part of the ear. How do you think the shape of the outer ear helps do these things?

Middle ear. The end of the tunnel in the outer ear is covered by a thin piece of skin. This piece of skin is called the *eardrum.* The eardrum is a part of the *middle ear.*

The middle ear is also made up of three small bones. As sounds hit the eardrum they make the eardrum vibrate. This makes the small bones vibrate. What do you think would happen if these bones did not vibrate?

You most likely have heard someone say that you should not put anything into your ears. Why do you think you should not do this?

Inner ear. Sounds are carried by the bones in the middle ear to a small opening. The sounds then go through this opening and into the *inner ear.*

Exploring on Your Own

Most sounds you hear reach your inner ear through your outer ear and middle ear. But some sounds can reach your inner ear in other ways. See if you can find out how. To do this, you might use reference books. Look under the heading *ear, hearing,* or *hearing aid.*

The inner ear is made up of many parts. The part that sounds move through is called the *cochlea* [KOH-klee-uh]. Look at the picture on this page. You will see how sounds move through the cochlea.

Connected to the cochlea is a large *nerve* [NURV]. This nerve picks up messages about sounds. It then carries these messages to the *brain*. Why do you think these messages must go to the brain?

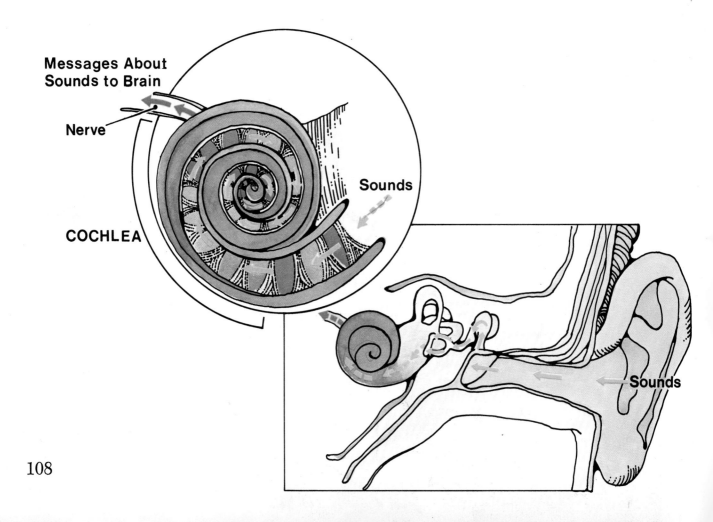

Messages About Sounds to Brain

Nerve

COCHLEA

Sounds

Sounds

Are two ears helpful?

Listen closely to the sounds around you. Now cover one ear with your hand. Listen again. Which way did you hear best?

As you may know, you need only one ear to hear some sounds. But when you listen with one ear, these sounds might be hard to understand. Why?

What if you thought you were not hearing as well as you should. What might you do? Why?

Hearing with both ears helps you understand sounds. But hearing with both ears also helps you tell where sounds are coming from. Why do you think this is so?

Why might it be important to be able to tell where sounds are coming from?

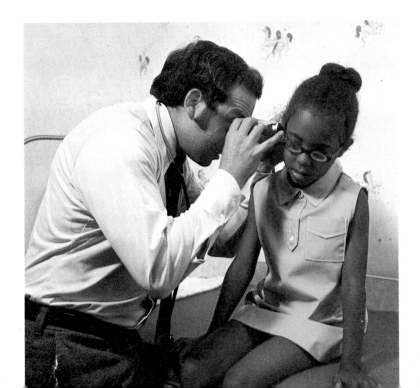

When a doctor gives a checkup, one thing the doctor does is look into your ears. Why do you think a doctor does this?

FINDING OUT

How can you tell where sounds are coming from?

You will need: 16 hard objects such as pencils, quiet room

▶ Give 8 people 2 objects each. Have them sit in a large circle.

▶ Sit in the middle of the circle. Cover your eyes with a blindfold and cover one ear with your hand.

▶ Have one person hit the objects together 2 or 3 times. Point to where you think the sound came from. Keep doing this until all the people have hit the objects together.

How many times did you guess right?

▶ Try it again. This time listen with both ears.

How many times did you guess right?
Which way did you find it easier to tell where the sounds were coming from?

A Second Look

1. What things does the outer ear do to help you hear sounds?
2. In what ways does hearing sounds with both ears help you?

Think about the many things around you that make sounds. Some things make high sounds. Some make low sounds. Why do you think this is so?

3 High and low sounds

What causes high and low sounds?

You most likely know that all sounds are made by things vibrating. But some things vibrate faster than others. The faster something vibrates, the higher the sound it makes. The slower something vibrates, the lower the sound it makes. What do you think makes some things vibrate faster than others?

Inside your voice box are some muscles. These muscles help your vocal cords make high and low sounds. What do you think these muscles do to help make high and low sounds?

Tightness of objects. As you may know, some things vibrate faster than others. One thing that can make this happen is their tightness.

Suppose you had a toy balloon filled with air. And suppose you were to stretch the mouth of the balloon by pulling on each side. If you let some air out of the balloon, it would make a sound. It would do this because the mouth of the balloon would be vibrating.

But what if you were to stretch the mouth of the balloon even more and let some air out of it. The mouth of the balloon would vibrate faster than before. Which time do you think the balloon would make the higher sound? Why?

What might you do to this drum so that it makes a higher sound? A lower sound?

112

FINDING OUT

Will tightening a rubber band change the sound it makes?

You will need: rubber band

► Hold one end of the rubber band between your teeth. Hold the other end with your thumb and first finger.
► Tighten the rubber band a little by pulling with your thumb and finger.
► Pluck the rubber band with a finger. Watch the rubber band and listen to the sound it makes.
► Tighten the rubber band a little more.
► Pluck the rubber band again. Watch the rubber band and listen to the sound it makes.

Did tightening the rubber band make the sound higher? If so, why?

Size of objects. There is something else that can make some things vibrate faster than others. This is their size.

What if you were to hit a big pan and then a little pan. The little pan would vibrate faster than the big pan. Which pan do you think would make the higher sound? Why?

Making music

Do you like to sing? Or play a musical instrument? Or maybe just listen to music? Music, like other sounds, is made by things vibrating.

Look at the picture on this page. How do you think music is made with each of these instruments?

String instruments. As you may know, some musical instruments have strings. When you pluck the strings, sounds are made.

Look at the picture of the guitar on this page. Which strings do you think would make high sounds? Why? Which strings do you think would make low sounds? Why? What might you do to change the sound of each string?

For You to Think About

Some string instruments are played most of the time by using a bow. A violin is one such instrument. What do you think the bow does to the strings of a violin?

Wind instruments. Have you ever blown into a toy whistle? Or across the top of a soda bottle? If so, you most likely know that you can make sounds this way. That is, air can be made to vibrate.

Air is used to make sounds in many musical instruments. Which of these instruments do you know of?

Which instruments shown do you think are wind instruments? How might you make sounds higher or lower with each of these wind instruments?

Suppose you had two empty soda bottles. One is big. The other is little. If you were to blow across the top of each bottle, the little bottle would make the higher sound. This is because the little bottle would have less air inside it than the big bottle. In which bottle do you think the air would be vibrating faster? How would you know?

FINDING OUT

How can you make music with soda bottles?

You will need: 8 empty soda bottles (all the same size), funnel

▶ Place the soda bottles in a line on a table.
▶ Blow across the top of each bottle.

What do you think is vibrating in the bottles to make sound? Why do you think all the bottles make about the same sound?

▶ Pour some water into one bottle.
▶ Blow across the top of this bottle and an empty bottle.

Which bottle made the higher sound? Why?

▶ Leave one bottle empty. Pour a different amount of water into all the other bottles. Place them in a line. Start with the bottle that makes the lowest sound.
▶ Try to play a song by blowing across the tops of the bottles.

If you wanted to make some of the sounds higher, what might you do?
If you wanted to make some of the sounds lower, what might you do?

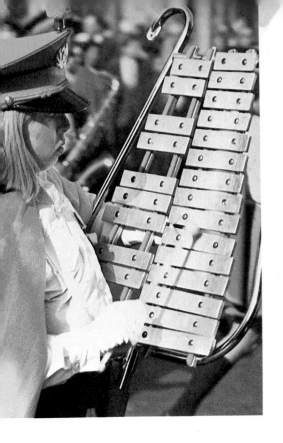

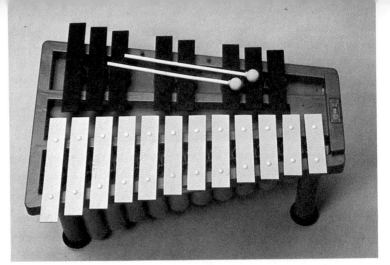

Percussion instruments. Some musical instruments make sounds when they are hit. These instruments are known as the *percussion* [pur-KUHSH-uhn] instruments.

Look at the instruments shown on this page. They make sounds when you hit the pieces of metal. If you wanted to make a high sound, which piece of metal might you hit? Why? Which ones might you hit to make a lower sound? Why?

What are some other percussion instruments you know of?

A Second Look

1. How might making something vibrate faster change the sound it makes?
2. What might make some things vibrate faster than other things?

Have you ever heard a bird sing? Or a bee buzz? Or maybe a cat meow? These sounds are only a few of the many animal sounds you may have heard. What are some other animal sounds you know of?

4 Animal sounds

How do some animals make sounds?

As you may know, there are many animals that make sounds. But all animals do not make sounds in the same way. In what ways do you think animals make sounds?

Vocal cords. Some animals make voice sounds in the same way you do. These animals use vocal cords to make sounds. Horses, cats, and birds are such animals. What other animals do you think use vocal cords to make sounds?

Other parts of the body. Some animals do not have vocal cords. Yet these animals make sounds.

You most likely have had a fly buzz around you. The buzzing sound you heard is made by the fly's wings vibrating. What are some other animals you know of that make sounds with their wings?

As you may know, a cricket makes a chirping sound. This sound is made when the cricket rubs its wing covers together. Look at the picture on this page. You can see the parts of the body a cricket uses to make sounds.

A rattlesnake uses a different part of its body to make sounds. Look at the picture of the rattlesnake on this page. How do you think a rattlesnake makes sounds?

Some interesting ears

Many animals have ears. Some animals have ears that are somewhat like yours.

Look at the pictures on this page. In what ways are these animals' ears like yours? In what ways are their ears different from yours?

Have you ever watched a dog's ears? If so, you most likely have seen that the ears sometimes lay flat. Other times the ears are straight up. What other animals do you know of that can move their ears?

Animals that move their ears can most often hear better than you can. How might being able to move their ears help animals hear better than you can?

Some animals have ears that are much different from yours. A katydid does not have outer ears. And its eardrums are on the outside of the body!

Look closely at the katydid's front leg in the picture below. You will see a small spot just below the "knee." This is one of the katydid's eardrums.

For You to Think About

A fish can hear many sounds. Yet it has only inner ears. How do you think sounds reach the inner ears of a fish?

Grasshoppers and frogs also have eardrums on the outside of their body. They look like the eardrums of the katydid. Look at the pictures of the grasshopper and frog on this page. Find their eardrums.

Why do you think it is important for animals to hear sounds?

A Second Look

1. In what ways do animals make sounds?
2. What helps some animals hear sounds better than you can?
3. What are some animals that do not have outer ears?

Workers Who Use Science

As you may know, you use your vocal cords to make sounds. You also use your lips, teeth, and tongue to change these sounds into words.

There are some people who have trouble making voice sounds. There are also some people who have trouble changing their voice sounds into words. These people have a speech problem.

There are many workers who help people with a speech problem. One such worker is called a *speech therapist* [THER-uh-puhst].

One thing a speech therapist does is try to find the cause of a speech problem. Another thing a speech therapist does is help some people learn how to make voice sounds better. A speech therapist also helps some people practice changing voice sounds into words.

To find out more about a speech therapist, try to find answers to these questions:

What else might a speech therapist do to help people with a speech problem?
What are some other causes of speech problems?
How can people without vocal cords be helped to speak?

Along with sources of your own, you may find that writing to the following source may help you: American Speech and Hearing Association, 9030 Old Georgetown Road, Washington, DC 20014.

This boy is learning to make better voice sounds. How might feeling the vibrations of his vocal cords help him do this?

Reviewing the Main Ideas

For something to make a sound, it or part of it
    must be vibrating.
You use your vocal cords to make voice sounds.
Sounds can travel in all directions.
Your ear is made up of three parts—the outer
    ear, middle ear, and inner ear.
Hearing sounds with both ears helps you under-
    stand sounds and tell where they come from.
The faster something vibrates, the higher the
    sound it makes.
Smaller things vibrate faster than larger things.
The tighter something is, the faster it vibrates.
Music, like other sounds, is made by things
    vibrating.
Some animals make sounds by using vocal cords.
Some animals make sounds with other parts of
    their body.

Reading About Science

Hutchins, Carleen M. *Who Will Drown the Sound?*
    New York: Coward, McCann & Geoghegan, Inc.,
    1972.
Podendorf, Illa. *Sounds All About.* Chicago:
    Childrens Press, Inc., 1970.
Scott, John M. *What Is Sound?* New York: Parents'
    Magazine Press, 1973.

Testing for Understanding

Ideas to Check

On your paper write *T* for each sentence below that is true. Write *F* for each one that is false.

1. Sounds can travel through many things.
2. Sounds travel in only two directions.
3. The faster something vibrates, the lower the sound it makes.
4. Air is used in some musical instruments to make sounds.
5. Animals that do not have vocal cords cannot make sounds.
6. Animals that can move their outer ears can most often hear better than you can.

Write on your paper the word or words that best fit in each blank below. Choose from these words:
outer ear, nerve, brain, vocal cords, eardrum, vibrating, inner ear.

Words to Use

1. The parts of your voice box which you use to make sounds are your ____.
2. The part of your ear that "catches" sounds is called your ____.
3. The thin piece of skin that covers one end of the small tunnel in the ear is called the ____.
4. Messages about sounds are picked up by a large ____ and sent to the brain.
5. For something to make a sound, it or part of it must be ____.

Having Fun with Science

What Am I?

1. I am a sound that is made only once. Yet I can be heard many times.
2. I am a drum, but you cannot beat on me.
3. I am a cord, but you cannot tie me in a knot.

Some words sound like what they mean. Two such words are *buzz* and *hum*. Make a list of some other words you know of that sound like what they mean.

Fun with Words

Things to Do

1. Make a rubber-band guitar. Get eight different-sized (thickness or length) rubber bands and a shoe-box lid. Put the rubber bands around the lid. Try playing some songs.

2. Make some sound effects. You might pour some rice or birdseed over Ping-Pong balls to make the sound of a hard rain. You might make the sound of an egg frying in a pan by slowly crumpling a small piece of cellophane. Try making some other sounds. See if people can tell what each sound is.

3. Catch a grasshopper, cricket, or frog. Try to find their eardrums. Use a magnifying glass to help you.

5 Water in Your Environment

1 Why is water important?

2 Where does water come from?

3 How is water made safe for people to drink?

4 How can water be used wisely?

In what ways do you use water?

Where does the water you use come from?

Do you think people will ever use up all the
water on earth? Why or why not?

1 Why is water important?

Have you ever taken care of a plant or an animal? If so, you may know that they need many things from their *environment* [ihn-VY-ruhn-muhnt], or surroundings. One of these things is air. Another thing plants and animals need is water. And you know that you need water. Why do you think living things need water?

How your body uses water

As you most likely know, your body is made up of many parts. Some of these parts are skin and blood. But most parts of your body are made up of still other things. One such thing is water. In fact, about two thirds of your weight is water.

Your body uses this water in many ways. In what ways do you think your body uses water?

To keep cool. What if you were to run or ride a bicycle on a very hot day. Your skin would most likely become wet with *sweat.* Sweat is mostly water.

Sweat helps cool your skin. This keeps your body from getting too warm. Do you think this is important? Why or why not?

Do you think you might feel thirsty more often after playing than after resting? Why or why not?

To change food. Your body also has other liquids which are mostly water. One such liquid is in your mouth. It is called *saliva* [suh-LY-vuh].

As you eat food, saliva is mixed with the food. This makes it easier for you to swallow food. But saliva also helps change some of the food you eat. Food must be changed so that it can be used by your body.

How else do you think your body uses water?

FINDING OUT

How can you tell that saliva helps change the food you eat?

You will need: piece of bread

▶ Place the piece of bread on your tongue. Do not chew it.

What does the bread taste like?

▶Now mix the bread with saliva. Do not chew it.

Does the bread now taste a little sweet? If so, what changed the bread so that it tastes sweet?

Some other ways water is used

As you may know, your body uses water to do many things. But water is also used by people in other ways.

To grow food. Do you like to eat corn? Oranges? Meat? If not, what are some foods you like to eat?

As you may know, all food is made from plants or animals. And plants and animals need water to stay alive. Because of this, people use water to help grow plants and animals that are used for food. What do you think might happen if there was not enough water for these plants and animals?

To clean things. "Wash the apple before you eat it." "Help me wash the dishes." "Don't forget to brush your teeth." You most likely have heard someone say these things. They point out that cleaning things is another way you use water. How do you think cleaning things helps you?

To make food. Have you ever cooked some rice? Or made some lemonade? If so, you most likely know that you use water to make these things. Water is also used to make other foods. What are some other foods you know of that water is used to make?

To make electricity. Water can be used to make *electricity* [ih-LEHK-TRIHS-uht-ee]. The picture on this page shows how water is used to make electricity.

You most likely use many things that are run by electricity. A toaster and a radio are such things. What other things do you use that are run by electricity?

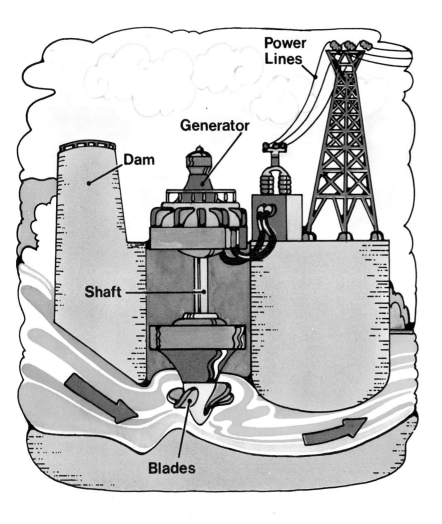

Rushing water from a dam can be used to make electricity. The water spins the blades and shaft of a machine called a generator. This spinning motion causes electricity to be made in the generator. How do you think this electricity gets to homes and other places?

To have fun. The pictures on this page and the next show people having fun with water. In what ways are they having fun with water? In what ways have you had fun with water?

For You to Think About

In this chapter, you may have read about many ways people use water. What other ways can you think of that people use water?

A Second Look

1. In what ways does your body use water?
2. What are some other ways people use water?
3. What are some things water is used to make?

2 Where does water come from?

What if you were to look at a map of the earth. You would see that most of the earth is covered with water. Some of this water is found in lakes and rivers. But most of the water on earth is found in oceans. This water is different from water in lakes and rivers. How might it be different?

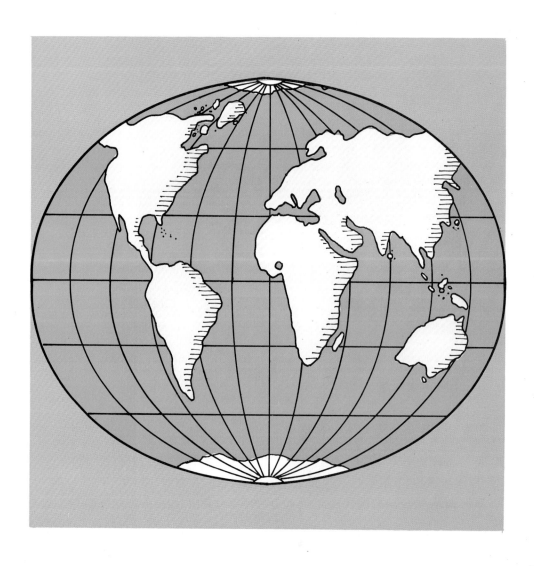

Salt water

Have you ever tasted ocean water? If so, you most likely know that it tastes salty. Ocean water has salt in it. Because of this, ocean water is called *salt water*.

Though most of the earth is covered with ocean water, you cannot drink it. Ocean water has so much salt in it that it would be harmful to you. It would also be harmful to many plants and animals.

FINDING OUT

In what way is salt water harmful to a plant?

You will need: 2 plants, salt

► Put both plants where they will get about the same amount of sunlight.

► Mix about 2 teaspoons of salt with a cup of fresh water. (This water may be thought of as ocean water although ocean water also has other things in it.)

► Water both plants every 2 or 3 days. Give one plant fresh water. Give the other plant salt water.

Was the salt water harmful to the plant? If so, how could you tell?

Fresh water

As you may know, most of the water on earth is salt water. But the water you use is called *fresh water*. Fresh water may have some salt in it, but not enough to be harmful to you.

Fresh water can be found in many places. Where might you find fresh water?

Lakes and rivers. Is there a lake near where you live? Or maybe a river? If so, the water you use may come from this lake or river.

The water in most lakes and rivers is fresh water. Where else might you find fresh water?

Wells. Some people live in places where there are no lakes or rivers close by. Yet these people have fresh water to use. They get their water from underground. This water is most often gotten from a well. How do you think this water gets underground?

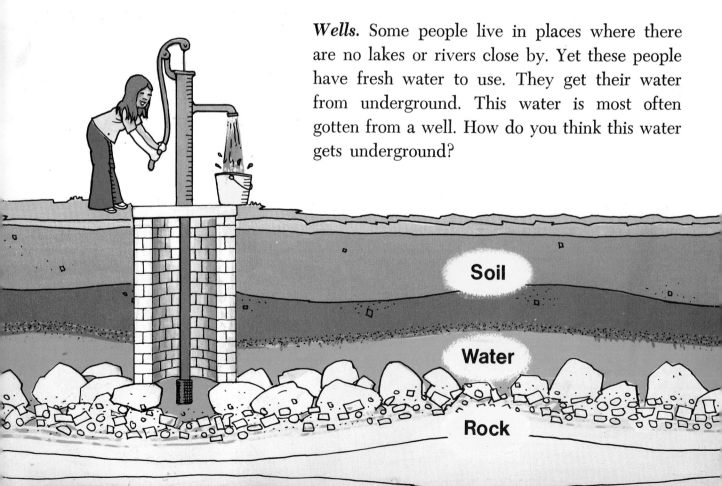

Soil

Water

Rock

Movement of water

Because people keep using water, more fresh water is needed to keep lakes, rivers, and wells filled. Where do you think this water comes from?

Rain and snow. You most likely have had to stop playing outside because of rain or snow. This may have made you unhappy. But rain and snow are important to you. Fresh water falls to earth as rain and snow. Rain and snow help keep lakes, rivers, and wells filled.

Evaporation. Water that falls as rain and snow is important to you. But how do you think water gets into the air to form rain and snow?

Have you ever noticed that a wet sidewalk soon dries? Or that a puddle of water soon goes away? Some of this water may go into the ground. But some of it *evaporates* [ih-VAP-uh-RAYTS]. That is, some of the water changes into a gas called *water vapor.* As water changes into water vapor, it goes into the air.

Exploring on Your Own

Some places have too much water. Other places have too little water. Having too much or too little water can cause problems for people. See if you can find out what some of these problems are. Also find out how these problems might be taken care of. You might use reference books to help you. Look under the headings *water, flood,* and *desert.*

141

MOVEMENT OF WATER

Clouds. Water vapor helps form clouds. Most clouds are formed over oceans. When ocean water evaporates, the salt is left behind.

Some of the clouds formed over oceans are blown over land. In time, the water vapor in these clouds is cooled. This makes the water vapor change into rain or snow. What things might happen if a place did not get rain or snow for a long time?

For You to Think About

As you may know, most of the water in the air has evaporated from oceans. But the amount of water in the oceans stays about the same. How do you think water gets back into oceans?

143

FINDING OUT

How can you show that water evaporates?

You will need: hot plate, 2 pans with handles, tray of ice cubes, glove

▶ Put some water in a pan. Heat the water, but do not boil it.

▶ Put the ice cubes in the other pan. Hold this pan about 20 centimetres (8 inches) above the other pan. Be sure to wear a glove on the hand holding the pan.

▶ Watch for small drops of water to form on the bottom of the pan you are holding.

What did the heat do to the water in the pan on the hot plate?
Where did the drops of water on the bottom of the pan with ice come from?
What do you think heats water on earth so that it evaporates?

A Second Look

1. How is ocean water different from fresh water?
2. Where can fresh water be found?
3. How does water get into the air?

What if you had two glasses of water. One glass is filled with water from a river. One glass is filled with water from a water faucet. In what way might the glasses of water look different from each other? Which glass of water would probably be safer to drink? Why?

3 How is water made safe for people to drink?

The need for clean water

You most likely know that fresh water can be found in lakes and rivers. But this water is not always clean. It may have things in it such as dirt and soap. These things are called *wastes*. This water may also have *germs* in it. Wastes and germs make water unclean. Where might wastes and germs come from?

Unclean water should not be used by people for drinking. Wastes and germs in the water can sometimes make people sick. These things can also hurt plants and animals. How might water be made safe for people to drink?

Looking at a water-treatment plant

Most cities and towns get their water from a lake or river. But before the water goes to homes and other places, it goes to a water-treatment plant. Here the water is made safe for people to drink. The picture found below and on the next page shows how this is done.

In a water-treatment plant, water is pumped into a chemical tank. Here, chemicals are mixed with the water. The water then goes into a settling tank. Here, the chemicals cause many of the wastes to fall to the bottom of the tank.

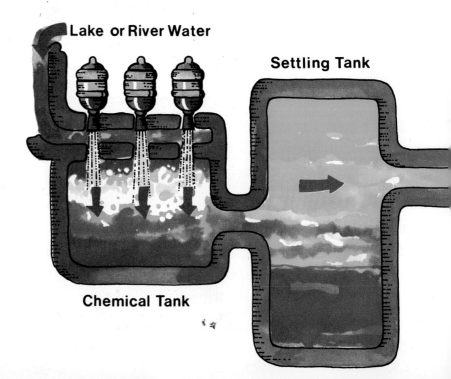

Lake or River Water

Settling Tank

Chemical Tank

146

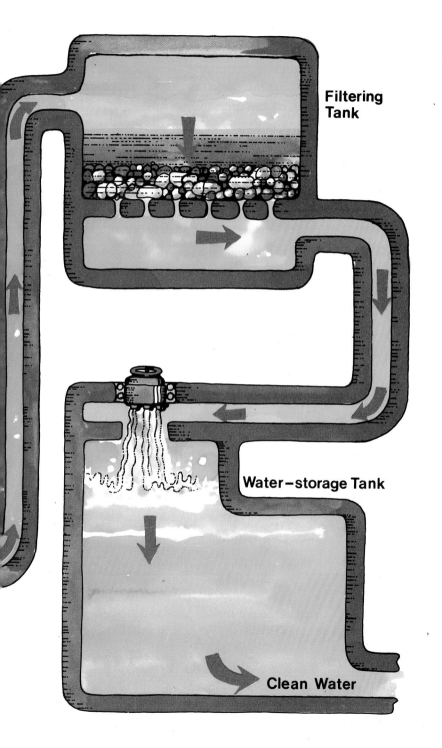

Filtering Tank

Water–storage Tank

Clean Water

Next, the water leaves the settling tank and goes into a filtering tank. Here, the water is filtered through sand and other things. How might this help clean the water?

After the water has been filtered, it goes into a water-storage tank. More chemicals are added to the water to kill germs. Why do you think this is important?

147

FINDING OUT

How does a filter help clean water?

You will need: empty milk carton, small glass jar, 2 or 3 pieces of charcoal, clean sand, cotton, muddy water

▶ Make some small holes in the bottom of the carton.
▶ Put some cotton inside the carton as shown.
▶ Then put some sand on top of the cotton.
▶ Crush the charcoal and put it on top of the sand.
▶ You have made a filter somewhat like those used in water-treatment plants.
▶ Hold the carton over the glass jar and pour some muddy water into the carton.

In what way does the filtered water look different from the muddy water?
In what way does a filter help clean muddy water?

After the water has been made safe for people to drink, it leaves the water-treatment plant. The water is pumped into large pipes. These pipes are underground. They carry water to homes and other buildings. The pipes may also carry some of the water to a water tower. A water tower is used to store water. Why might it be important to store water?

Water Tower

Pumping Station

Water-treatment Plant

HOW WATER GETS TO MANY PLACES

A Second Look

1. What things may make lake and river water unclean?
2. What does a water-treatment plant do?
3. How does clean water get to homes and other places?

4 How can water be used wisely?

As you may know, there are more people living now than ever before. Therefore, more fresh water is being used now than ever before. To make sure there will be enough water, it is important for people to use water wisely. In what ways might people use water wisely?

Saving water

The pictures on this page show some people using water. Which person is saving water? How is that person saving water?

The table on this page shows some things people clean with water. The table also shows how much water might be used to clean these things. What might people do to save water when washing a car? When washing dishes? When cleaning their body?

How else might people save water?

Some Ways People Can Save Water

Use of water	Amount of water used	
	litres	(gallons)
Washing a car		
with a hose and running water	76	(20)
with a bucket of water	19	(5)
Washing dishes		
with a dishwashing machine	57	(15)
by hand	19	(5)
Cleaning their body		
by taking a bath	133	(35)
by taking a shower	95	(25)

Controlling water pollution

As you may know, people use water in many ways. After people use water, it often has wastes and germs in it. For years many cities and factories have emptied this water into lakes and rivers. Because of this, the water in lakes and rivers has become *polluted* [puh-LOOT-uhd]. That is, the water has become unclean.

Many cities and factories now treat water before it is put back into lakes and rivers. To do this, they take some of the wastes and germs out of the water. This helps to control water pollution. Do you think this is important? Why or why not?

The pictures on these pages show polluted water. What might people do to help stop water pollution?

Changing salt water into fresh water

In time, there may be even more people living than there are now. So the need for water will be even greater. People may have to get their water from oceans. To do this, they will have to change salt water into fresh water.

The pictures on this page show one way salt water can be changed into fresh water. Do you think it is important to keep oceans from becoming polluted? Why or why not?

This girl is trying to change salt water into fresh water. She is doing this by freezing the salt water. Of course, much more salt water would have to be frozen to supply a town with fresh water! See if you can change salt water into fresh water in this way.

FINDING OUT

How can you change salt water into fresh water?

You will need: salt, drinking glass, clear plastic kitchen wrap, rubber band, black paper

▶ Mix about 2 teaspoons of salt with a glass of water.

▶ Stretch a piece of plastic kitchen wrap tightly over the top of the glass. Put a rubber band around the glass to hold the wrap in place.

▶ Place the glass on a piece of black paper in the sunlight near a window.

▶ After about an hour you should see some water on the underside of the plastic wrap. Remove the wrap from the glass. Taste the water on the wrap and in the glass.

Which water was fresh water?
Do you think the sun helped change the salt water into fresh water? If so, how?

A Second Look

1. Why is it important for people to use water wisely?
2. What are some cities and factories doing to help control water pollution?
3. Why is being able to change salt water into fresh water important?

Workers Who Use Science

It is important for people to use water wisely. Because of this, there are many workers who study water and look for ways to use water wisely. One such worker is a *hydrologist* [hy-DRAHL-uh-juhst].

One thing a hydrologist does is study the ground in certain places. A hydrologist finds out how much water might be underground in those places. This helps people know where to dig for a well.

Another thing a hydrologist does is help people find ways of storing water. A hydrologist might study a river to find the best place to build a dam. A dam can be used to help store water for a city.

To find out more about how a hydrologist helps people use water wisely, try to find the answers to these questions:

How might the work of a hydrologist be helpful to farmers in growing food?
How might the work of a hydrologist be helpful to people living near a river that often floods?
How else might the work of a hydrologist be helpful to people?

Along with sources of your own, you might find that writing to the following source may help you: American Geological Institute, 2201 M. Street, N.W., Washington, DC 20037.

A farmer wants to know how deep to drill for water in this place. This hydrologist is using a special machine to find out.

Reviewing the Main Ideas

Some of the ways your body uses water are to keep
cool and change the food you eat.

People also use water to grow food, clean things,
make things, and have fun.

Most of the water on earth is found in oceans.
Ocean water is salt water.

The water you use is fresh water. Fresh water can
be found in wells and in most lakes and rivers.

When water evaporates, it changes into water vapor
and goes into the air. Water vapor helps form
clouds.

When water vapor in clouds is cooled, it changes
into rain or snow.

A water-treatment plant makes water safe for people
to drink.

People can use water wisely by saving water,
controlling water pollution, and changing salt
water into fresh water.

Reading About Science

Gans, Roma. *Water for Dinosaurs & You*. New York:
Thomas Y. Crowell Company, 1973.

Lefkowitz, R. J. *Water for Today & Tomorrow*. New
York: Parents' Magazine Press, 1973.

Russell, Helen R. *Water: A Field Trip Guide*.
Boston: Little, Brown & Company, 1973.

Testing for Understanding

On your paper write *T* for each sentence below that is true. Write *F* for each sentence that is false.

1. Most of the water on earth is fresh water.
2. Plants and animals need water to stay alive.
3. Water can be used to make electricity.
4. Water vapor helps form clouds.
5. Saving water is one way people can use water wisely.
6. When water vapor in clouds is warmed, it is changed into rain or snow.

Write on your paper the word or words that best fit in each blank below. Choose from these words: *evaporates, saliva, fresh water, water-treatment plant, salt water, polluted, sweat, germs.*

1. When you eat food, ____ helps change the food so that it can be used by your body.
2. When your body gets too warm, ____ from your body helps cool your skin.
3. Ocean water is also called ____.
4. The water you drink and use in many other ways is called ____.
5. A ____ makes water safe for people to drink.
6. When water ____, it changes into a gas and goes into the air.

Having Fun with Science

1. When you take a warm bath or shower, you may have noticed that the mirror or window in the bathroom gets "cloudy." Why does this happen?
2. Sometimes a city water pipe may break. After the pipe has been fixed, people may be asked to boil the water that comes into their home. Why?

Some words can be written in a way that shows their meaning.

Fun with Words

EVAPORATE CLOUDS

Draw some other words about water in a way that shows their meaning.

Things to Do

1. Most homes have a water meter. It measures how much water is used in your home. Find where the meter is in your home. Find out how much water your family uses in a month and how much it costs. Ask someone in your family to help you.

2. Think of as many ways as you can to change salt water into fresh water. You might try freezing salt water. You might try filtering it. Find out which way is best.

6 Location, Motion, and Force

1 Where are you?

2 Moving along

3 What makes it move?

Do you think what Tom said was helpful
in finding the ball? Why or why not?

When have you had to tell someone where
to find something? What did you say
to that person?

1 Where are you?

Name some of the places where you have been yesterday and today. Have you been to a park? A friend's house? A store? Where are you now?

The place where you are at any time is your *location* [loh-KAY-shuhn]. Why do you think it is important to know your location? When might it be important to know the location of things around you?

Using reference objects

What if you wanted to visit a new friend. You would have to know the location of your friend's house. To help you find the house, your friend might say, "My house is the white house across from Bell School and next to Brown's Store." Bell School and Brown's Store are used to help tell where the house is. Things that are used to help tell about the location of something are called *reference objects*.

Think about the location of the place where you live. What reference objects would you use to help tell about its location?

Look around you and choose something as a reference object. What is your location? Are you *in front* of the object or *behind* it? Are you *near* the object or *far* from it? What other words might you use to help tell about your location?

For You to Think About

Suppose you lost your way while traveling someplace. What would you do, and why?

Knowing how near or how far

As was said, *near* and *far* are words you might use to help tell about your location. But there are some times when you need to know just *how near* or *how far* something is from you. When are some of these times?

The map on the next page shows the location of some of the places in a town. Look at the map and find the place marked "Your Home." How

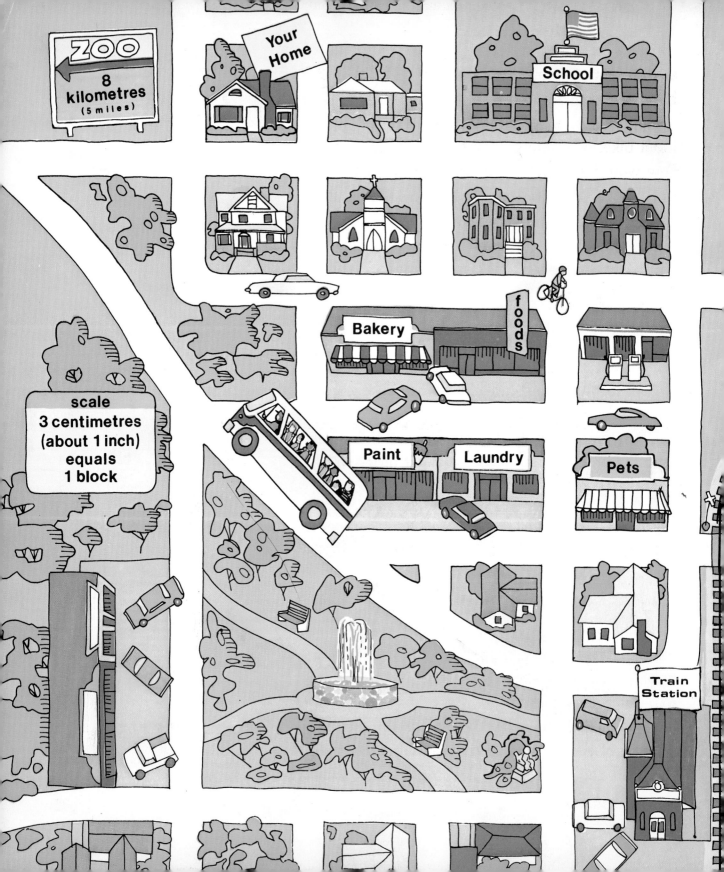

far is it from "Your Home" to the zoo? The pet shop? The school? The train station?

Suppose you had to choose whether to walk, ride a bike, or ride a bus to each of these places. How would you get to the zoo? Why? The pet store? Why? The school? Why? The train station? Why?

FINDING OUT

What places in your neighborhood are important to you?

You will need: paper, pencil, crayons

▶ Using the pencil, draw a map of your neighborhood. Be sure to show the place where you live.
▶ Show some other places in your neighborhood that are important to you.

Why are they important?

▶ Label and color the important places that are on your map.
▶ Draw a line to show how you get to each of these places from where you live.

To which of these places do you walk? Ride a bike? Ride in a car?

Look at the pictures on this page. What are the children doing? Why is it important for these children to know just how far something is from them?

A Second Look

1. What is meant by your location?
2. When might you use reference objects?
3. What are some words that help tell about the location of something?

How many times have you moved, or changed your location, today? What things do you see moving as you look around you? Everything that is moving is said to be in *motion* [MOH-shuhn].

You move many things each day. What are some things you might want to move? Why might you want to move them?

2 Moving along

Straight or curved?

Whenever something is in motion, it may move in a straight line. Or, it may move in a curved line. The pictures on this page show some things in motion. Which things are moving in a straight line? Which things are moving in a curved line?

What other things can you think of that move in a straight line? What other things can you think of that move in a curved line?

A funny thing about motion

Can you ever be moving and not moving at the same time? Think back to a time when you were riding in a car or bus. The car or bus was moving you from one location to another. But you were sitting still in your seat as you rode along.

When are some other times you or something else might be moving and not moving?

The girl in this picture is both moving and not moving. How can this be so?

As you may know, the earth is always moving around the sun. So, everything on earth is always moving around the sun. It may not seem like you are moving. But you are moving along with the earth. Why does it seem like you are not moving?

Starting and stopping

The pictures on this page show something else about motion. That is, things will not move unless something starts them moving. And things will keep moving unless something stops them.

Look at the first picture. Could the wagon start to move by itself? Why or why not? What are some other ways things might start moving?

Now look at the second picture. What do you think will happen when the wagon gets to the bottom of the hill? Why? What are some other ways things might stop moving?

FINDING OUT

How can you keep a yo-yo moving?

You will need: yo-yo

▶ Spin the yo-yo down its string. Wait until it stops spinning.

What started the yo-yo spinning?
What stopped it from spinning?

▶ Spin the yo-yo down its string again.
▶ Try to make the yo-yo move up and down on its string 3 or 4 times.

What did you have to do to keep the yo-yo moving up and down?

171

Many times the police use tracks of cars to find out how an accident happened. How do you think these tracks might help them do this?

Where did they go?

You can often find out much about the way things move by looking at the *tracks,* or marks, they leave.

The picture on this page shows some animal tracks. Which of the animals came from the house? Which of them came from the tree? Which animals came from over the hill? What else can you find out by looking at the tracks?

The boy in the top picture on the next page is looking for his brother and his dog. What can he find out from looking at their tracks? When have you used tracks to find something?

Look at the bottom picture on the next page. See how many tracks you can find.

What other things can you think of that show tracks?

A Second Look

1. What are two ways in which something may move?
2. How can something be moving and not moving at the same time?
3. How might tracks be helpful to you?

3 What makes it move?

Each day you see many things around you move. Whenever something moves, it moves because of a *force*. A force is a push or a pull. A force is needed to make a train's wheels move around and around. A force is needed to make a ball move through the air. A force is needed to make a leaf fall from a tree. Where might the force to make each of these things move come from?

A force from you

Think about running, jumping, or throwing a ball. Whenever you do these things, you are moving parts of your body. When you move any part of your body, you are using a force. That force is coming from your *muscles* [MUHS-uhlz]. What muscles do you think the girl pictured on page 174 is using?

Look at the picture at the right. Put your hand on your arm just like the boy in the picture is doing. Bend your arm toward you. Where is the force to move your arm coming from? Name some other times when you use the force from your arm muscle.

How are the children in the picture below using force from their muscles? Which muscles are they using? Which side do you think will win? Why?

Help from machines

Forces which move things may also come from *machines*. The machines you see in these pictures are being used to move things. Why is each machine able to move something? What are some other machines that are used to move things?

Down it goes

Think back to the first time you were on roller skates. Or the first time you rode a bike. Did you fall a few times? If so, you fell because of a force called *gravity* [GRAV-uht-ee]. Gravity is a force that pulls everything toward the earth. Wherever you are right now, gravity is pulling on you. What do you think would happen if there were no gravity on the earth?

FINDING OUT

How can you measure the force of gravity on different things?

You will need: scale (such as a bathroom scale or a spring scale), 3 or 4 heavy things such as books or rocks

▶ Weigh each thing with the scale. Write down the weight of each thing. (The weight shows how much the force of gravity is pulling on each thing.)

▶ Guess the weight of some other things around you. Weigh them.

How close were your guesses?
When might you need to know just how much something weighs?

The children in the picture on this page are having fun with their sleds. They just rode down the hill. If they want to get back to the top of the hill they must walk up and pull their sleds. To get up the hill, they must pull harder than the earth's gravity is pulling down on them and their sleds.

When they get to the top of the hill, they will get on their sleds and ride down again. Gravity will pull them down. When have you used the earth's gravity to move something?

Using magnets

Have you ever seen or used a *magnet* [MAG-nuht]? If so, you may know that force from a magnet can move things.

Look at the picture on this page. Which of the things in the picture will the magnet move? Why? What are some other things a magnet can move? Get a magnet. Try moving some things with your magnet.

Exploring on Your Own

Though something may move because of a force, it may also slow down or stop moving because of a force. One such force is called *friction*. Find out what causes friction. You may want to use reference books to help you. Name some times when friction may slow something down or stop it from moving.

What force is it?

As you may know, forces move many things. Look at the picture below. What things do you think are moving? What force do you think is making each of them move?

FINDING OUT

What are some other forces that can move things?

You will need: 2 marbles, table

▶ Place one of the marbles in the middle of the table.
▶ Try to blow the marble off the end of the table.

What force did you use to make the marble move?

▶ Put the marble back in the middle of the table.
▶ Roll the other marble so it hits this marble.

Where did the force that moved the marble in the middle of the table come from?
Name some other times when a moving object will make something else move.

A Second Look

1. What is a force?
2. Where does the force that helps you lift a book come from?
3. What is gravity, and what does it do?

Workers Who Use Science

Every day you do things that have to do with location, motion, and force. You may move something from one place to another. You may take a ride across town. There are some workers who must know many things about location, motion, and force. *Airplane pilots* are such workers.

Airplane pilots must know how to find the location of many places when they are flying an airplane. To do this, they use special maps. Pilots must make sure that the airplane is moving along the right path. To do this, they must know how to use a radio. They must also know how to guide the airplane through strong wind forces.

To find out more about airplane pilots, try to find answers to these questions:

What is radar, and how is it helpful to pilots?
What are some other things pilots use to help them find the location of places?
What other forces must pilots know about?

Along with sources of your own, writing to the following places may help you: Air Transport Association of America, 1000 Connecticut Ave., N.W., Washington, DC 20036. International Air Line Pilots Association, 55th St. and Cicero Ave., Chicago, Illinois 60638.

This airplane pilot is checking many things in the airplane before takeoff. What might some of these things be?

Reviewing the Main Ideas

The place where you are at any time is your location.

Reference objects are used to help tell about the
location of something.

There are times when it is important to know just
how near or how far something is from you.

When something is in motion, it may move in a
straight line. Or, it may move in a curved line.

Things will not move unless something starts them
moving. And things will keep moving unless
something stops them.

You can find out about the way some things move
by looking at their tracks.

Whenever something moves, it moves because of a
force.

Force can come from muscles, machines, gravity,
or magnets.

Reading About Science

Bendick, Jeanne. *Why Things Work: A Book About
Energy.* New York: Parents' Magazine Press, 1972.

Bradley, Franklyn. *Gravity Is a Mystery.* New York:
Thos. Y. Crowell Co., 1970.

Kirn, Ann. *How to Be a Nature Detective.* New York:
G. P. Putnam's Sons, 1969.

Ubell, Earl. *The World of Push and Pull.* New York:
Atheneum Publishers, 1964.

Testing for Understanding

Ideas to Check

On your paper write *T* for each sentence below that is true. Write *F* for each sentence that is false.

1. Reference objects are often used to help tell about the location of something.
2. *Near* and *far* are words that help tell about the location of something.
3. All things move in a straight line.
4. Many animals show tracks.
5. When you move any part of your body, you are using a force.
6. Things will not move unless something starts them moving.

Write on your paper the word that best fits in each blank below. Choose from these words: *map, motion, gravity, location, earth, force, machine, tracks.*

Words to Use

1. The ____ is always moving around the sun.
2. The **force** from a ____ can move things.
3. A ____ can be used to help find the location of something.
4. A ____ is a push or a pull.
5. Where you are right now is your ____.
6. The marks that things may leave when they move are known as ____.

Having Fun with Science

What Am I?

1. I will be anywhere you happen to be.
2. I never stop moving. And you move along with me.

Fun with Words

Think of a word that means location.
It sounds like *race* and *face.*

Think of a word that means moving.
It sounds like *lotion* and *potion.*

Think of a word that means a push or a pull.
It sounds like *horse* and *course.*

Mystery Games

1. Play a mystery game with a group of people. Have someone go out of the room. Have someone else point to an object in the room. Have the first person come back into the room and guess the mystery object. This person must use reference objects to guess the mystery object. This person might ask, "Is it on *top* of the *table?* Or *behind* the *door?*"

2. Get some clay. Press it out like a pancake. Make some tracks in the clay with something such as a fork. Have other people try to guess what you used to make the tracks.

Glossary-Index

One of the purposes of this glossary-index is to help you pronounce and understand certain words in this book. Another purpose is to help you find out about topics in this book that may interest you. You can find out about a topic by turning to the page or pages given at the end of each topic that is listed.

In this glossary-index, the syllables of a word are separated by a space. This can help you say the word. A special spelling may follow a word. This spelling always appears in [ ]. This spelling can also help you say the word. When a word has two or more syllables, one syllable is stressed more than others. This syllable is always spelled with large capital letters, as in the word *gravity* [GRAV-uht-ee]. Syllables that are not stressed are always spelled with small letters. Sometimes a word has one or more syllables that are stressed, but not so much as the syllable spelled with large capital letters. Those syllables are spelled with small capital letters, as in the word *electricity* [ih-LEHK-TRIHS-uht-ee]. Words of only one syllable are also spelled with small capital letters, as in the word *nerve* [NURV].

Sometimes a syllable in a special spelling is placed inside ( ), as in the word *mineral* [MIHN(-uh)-ruhl]. This means that some people say the syllable when they say the word, but some people do not.

Below is a list of the letters and letter groups used for the special spellings. Across from each letter or letter group, you can read how most people say the letter or letter group.

Letter or letter group	Say like
a	*a* in *hat* [HAT]
ah	*a* in *father* [FAHTH-ur] and *o* in *hot* [HAHT]
aw	*a* in *all* [AWL] and *o* in *order* [AWRD-ur]
ay	*a* in *face* [FAYS]
ch	*ch* in *child* [CHYLD] and in *much* [MUHCH]
ee	*e* in *equal* [EE-kwuhl]
eh	*e* in *let* [LEHT]
eye	the first *i* in *iris* [EYE-ruhs]
g	*g* in *go* [GOH]
ih	*i* in *hit* [HIHT]
oh	*o* in *open* [OH-puhn]

Letter or letter group	Say like
oo	*oo* in *food* [FOOD] and *u* in *rule* [ROOL]
ow	*ou* in *out* [OWT]
oy	*oi* in *voice* [VOYS]
s	*s* in *say* [SAY]
sh	*sh* in *she* [SHEE]
u	*u* in *put* [PUT] and *oo* in *foot* [FUT]
uh	*u* in *cup* [KUHP]
ur	*er* in *term* [TURM] and *ir* in *sir* [SUR]
y	*i* in *nice* [NYS]
z	*s* in *degrees* [dih-GREEZ]
zh	*s* in *treasure* [TREHZH-ur]

(Acknowledgments continued from page 2)

Alpha Photo Associates/*John Fay*, 143 (bottom). Artstreet: 13 (top left and bottom right), 26, 71 (top right), 79, 82, 83, 85 (left), 92, 116, 152, 153. Artstreet/*Whitney Lilane*, 9. Authenticated News Int., 66. California Academy of Science/*E. S. Ross:* 120 (top), 122, 123 (right).   A. Devaney, Inc., 137 (bottom). A. Devaney, Inc./*Gene Johnson*, 28. DeWys, Inc., 176 (left). DeWys, Inc./*Martin W. Vanderwall*, 118 (left). DeWys, Inc./*Andre Picou*, 119 (top). DeWys, Inc./*Neil Graham*, 121 (left). Editorial Photocolor Archives/*Peter Vadnai:* 104 (both), 111. Editorial Photocolor Archives/*David H. Thompson*, 136 (left). *John D. Firestone:* 90, 91, 109. Freelance Photographers Guild, 48. Freelance Photographers Guild/*J. W. Thompson*, 41 (left). Frontier Airlines, 182. Grant Heilman: 13 (bottom left), 18, 130 (top), 133. Grant Heilman/*S. Rannels*, 11. Grant Heilman/*Runk/Schoenberger*, 12. Grant Heilman/*George H. Harrison*, 80 (bottom). Grant Heilman/*Alan Pitcairn*, 130 (bottom). Illinois State Geological Survey, 156. Monkmeyer Press Photo Service: 57 (left), 136 (bottom right). Monkmeyer Press Photo Service/*Hugh Rogers*, 36 (top left). Monkmeyer Press Photo Service/*Helmut Hendrik*, 57 (right). Monkmeyer Press Photo Service/*Freda Leinwand*, 98. Monkmeyer Press Photo Service/*Bendick Assoc.*, 119 (right). Monkmeyer Press Photo Service/*John G. O'Connor*, 168 (right). Monkmeyer Press Photo Service/*Mimi Forsyth*, 169. Monkmeyer Press Photo Service/*Merrim*, 174. *Tom Navta:* 8 (left), 85 (right), 137 (top), 176 (bottom right). Photo Research Int.: 8 (bottom right), 47, 71 (top left and bottom left), 72 (right), 81, 123 (left), 136 (top right), 166 (left), 175 (left). Photo Research Int./*Emil Muench*, 121 (top center). Photo Research Int./*C. Gaynor:* 168 (bottom left), 176 (top right). *G. R. Roberts:* 34 (right), 44, 53. Tom Stack and Associates/*Gene Haman*, 36 (top right). Tom Stack and Associates/*Stephen Dalton*, 38. Tom Stack and Associates/*A. Blueman*, 40. Tom Stack and Associates/*F. Greenaway*, 49. Tom Stack and Associates/*Warren Garst:* 50 (right), 55. Tom Stack and Associates/*Tom Meyers*, 60. Sunrise Photofeatures/*Rohn Engh*, 178. U.S. Steel Corporation, 71 (bottom right). Van Cleve Photography/*James R. Simon*, 35. Van Cleve Photography/*Leonard Lee Rue III*, 43. Van Cleve Photography/*William H. Stribling*, 50 (left). Van Cleve Photography/*Rohn Engh*, 78. Van Cleve Photography/*George Marcassidy*, 119 (left). Van Cleve Photography/*James R. Simon*, 120 (bottom). Van Cleve Photography/*Barbara Van Cleve:* 131, 166 (right). Van Cleve Photography/*Ossy Werner*, 145. Van Cleve Photography/*George Curtisinger*, 168 (top left). Zefa/*Werner H. Müller*, 70. Zefa/*E. Hummel*, 72 (left). Zefa/*H. Lütticke*, 80 (top). Zefa/*Dr. Heydemann-Müller*, 121 (right). Zefa/*K. Paysan*, 121 (bottom center).